Kendo UI Cookbook

Over 50 recipes to help you rapidly build rich and dynamic user interfaces for web and mobile platforms

Sagar Ganatra

[PACKT] open source*
PUBLISHING   community experience distilled

BIRMINGHAM - MUMBAI

Kendo UI Cookbook

First published: June 2014

Production reference: 1180614

Published by Packt Publishing Ltd.
Livery Place
35 Livery Street
Birmingham B3 2PB, UK.

ISBN 978-1-78398-000-0

www.packtpub.com

Cover image by Faiz F (faizfattohi@gmail.com)

Credits

Author

Sagar Ganatra

Reviewers

Sergey N. Bolshchikov

Austin Christenberry

David J. McClelland

Omkar Patil

Radu Poenaru

Acquisition Editor

Kevin Colaco

Content Development Editor

Vaibhav Pawar

Technical Editors

Taabish Khan

Pooja Nair

Nikhil Potdukhe

Copy Editor

Stuti Srivastava

Project Coordinator

Sanchita Mandal

Proofreaders

Simran Bhogal

Ameesha Green

Lawrence Herman

Joanna McMahon

Indexer

Mariammal Chettiyar

Production Coordinator

Komal Ramchandani

Cover Work

Komal Ramchandani

About the Author

Sagar Ganatra is a frontend architect from Bangalore, India. He is an expert in building web applications using modern web technologies such as HTML5, CSS3, Object-Oriented JavaScript, Kendo UI, jQuery, and JavaScript frameworks such as BackboneJS, RequireJS, and AngularJS. He also writes about these technologies in his blog at http://www.sagarganatra.com/. This is his second book; his previous book is *Instant Kendo UI Mobile*, *Packt Publishing*, which was published in 2013. When he is not coding, he enjoys writing short stories, swimming, and reading books.

I dedicate this book to my extraordinary parents, Tara Ganatra and Harshad Rai Ganatra, two of the greatest and wisest teachers in my life.

I also dedicate this book to my brother, Santosh Ganatra, and sister-in-law, Nisha Ganatra, for always standing by my side and encouraging me to write this book.

About the Reviewers

Sergey N. Bolshchikov is a senior frontend engineer at New ProImage (Agfa), working on a large-scale, client-side application of workflow systems software for publishing houses. He also serves as a co-organizer of the Ember-IL meet-up group in Tel Aviv, Israel. He holds an MSc degree in Information Systems from Technion – Israel Institute of Technology.

Austin Christenberry has experience working with technologies such as ASP.NET, T-SQL, Knockout.js, and Kendo UI. He currently works for Credera, a management and technology solutions firm based in Dallas, Texas. He graduated from Baylor University in Waco, Texas, in 2012 with a Bachelor of Science degree in Applied Mathematics. In his free time, he enjoys playing tennis and discovering new shows on Netflix.

> I would like to thank my beautiful wife, Len, for supporting me in reviewing this book, along with everything else I do.

David J. McClelland has been creating cutting-edge software and content that bridges design, development, and information for over 20 years. He is currently a Principle User Interface Engineer developing software to manage distributed devices via the cloud. He has been a technical reviewer for *Instant Kendo UI Mobile*, *Sagar Ganatra*, *Packt Publishing*.

> I would like to thank my family for encouraging my many technical and artistic interests.

Omkar Patil is currently working as a senior architect in the Global Technology and Architecture group of SunGard. He has 14 years experience in architecture, design, and development of web applications. Starting with server-side Enterprise Java, he has shifted focus to frontend development of web and mobile applications in the last few years. His current skill set consists of JavaScript, jQuery, Kendo UI, AngularJS, and Node.js. In his spare time, he enjoys reading, playing with new technologies, and contributing to open source software. He is a committer of the Angular-Kendo project that integrates Kendo UI with AngularJS (`https://github.com/kendo-labs/angular-kendo`).

I would like to thank my wife, Anu, for her support and encouragement over the past 12 years. I would also like to mention my daughter, Rewa, who at seven years of age, has already started coding and keeps me on my toes with her programming questions.

Radu Poenaru has over 12 years experience in software engineering, ranging from desktop to web and mobile applications. As a freelancer based in Frankfurt, Germany, he focuses his skills to deliver solutions for the complete life cycle of a website, including architecture and user experience—in the frontend using HTML5 and CSS3 and enhanced by JavaScript libraries such as jQuery, Knockout.js, Kendo UI, AngularJS, RequireJS, Modernizr, and Bootstrap; and in the backend using ASP.NET, MVC pattern (including Single-Page applications), Entity Framework, and Microsoft SQL. He discusses these and other software subjects on his blog at `http://www.radupoenaru.com` or on his company's website at `http://www.itbrainiacs.com`.

www.PacktPub.com

Support files, eBooks, discount offers, and more

You might want to visit www.PacktPub.com for support files and downloads related to your book.

Did you know that Packt offers eBook versions of every book published, with PDF and ePub files available? You can upgrade to the eBook version at www.PacktPub.com and as a print book customer, you are entitled to a discount on the eBook copy. Get in touch with us at service@packtpub.com for more details.

At www.PacktPub.com, you can also read a collection of free technical articles, sign up for a range of free newsletters, and receive exclusive discounts and offers on Packt books and eBooks.

http://PacktLib.PacktPub.com

Do you need instant solutions to your IT questions? PacktLib is Packt's online digital book library. Here, you can access, read, and search across Packt's entire library of books.

Why Subscribe?

- Fully searchable across every book published by Packt
- Copy and paste, print, and bookmark content
- On demand and accessible via web browser

Free Access for Packt account holders

If you have an account with Packt at www.PacktPub.com, you can use this to access PacktLib today and view nine entirely free books. Simply use your login credentials for immediate access.

Table of Contents

Preface   1

Chapter 1: The Kendo UI Application Framework   7
Introduction   7
Using client-side templates to generate HTML markup from a JSON data   8
Creating a two-way binding between View elements and JavaScript
objects using the Model View ViewModel (MVVM) pattern   12
Using Source and Template binding with ViewModels to generate
HTML content   16
Validating user input using the built-in Validator   19

Chapter 2: The Kendo UI Grid   23
Introduction   23
Creating a Grid view and displaying tabular data   23
Displaying data from a local or remote DataSource component in a Grid view   28
Sorting data in a Grid using a selected column   32
Using filters to display data that matches certain criteria in the Grid   35
Creating, updating, and deleting in Grid   39
Using the virtualization mechanism to improve the performance of the Grid   43
Customizing the look and feel of the Grid   46

Chapter 3: Kendo UI TreeView   49
Introduction   49
Using a TreeView widget to display a directory structure   49
Using the drag and drop feature to move elements in TreeView   55
Using checkboxes to select nodes in TreeView   58
Associating icons with labels in TreeView   62

Chapter 4: Kendo UI Editor   65

Introduction   65
Creating a WYSIWYG Editor using the kendoEditor function   65
Adding and removing tools in the Editor toolset   67
Using the image browser tool to insert images into the Editor   70

Chapter 5: Kendo UI PanelBar   77

Introduction   77
Creating a PanelBar   77
Loading the content of a PanelBar using Ajax   83
Binding the PanelBar to a DataSource object   86
Customizing the PanelBar   88

Chapter 6: Kendo UI File Uploader   91

Introduction   91
Using the file uploader to upload files to the server   91
Uploading files to the server asynchronously   94
Listening to file upload events   98

Chapter 7: Kendo UI Window   101

Introduction   101
Displaying a pop up and blocking the user interaction by configuring it as
a modal window   102
Customizing the look and feel of the window and including action buttons   105
Using the Window API to act on a window object   108

Chapter 8: Kendo UI Mobile Framework   111

Introduction   111
Creating a layout and adding views to the layout   112
Setting the initial layout and view when initializing the application   117
Using the Application object to navigate to various views   121
Adding touch events to your mobile application   126

Chapter 9: Kendo UI Mobile Widgets   129

Introduction   129
Creating a list using a ListView widget   130
Binding the ListView widget to a DataSource object   134
Fixing the headers when the user scrolls through the list   137
Filtering the elements in ListView   139
Building a hierarchical list using the ListView widget   143
Building an endless scrolling list   148
Showing a list of actions that can be performed using the
ActionSheet widget   150

Using the ScrollView widget to navigate through a collection of pictures   153
Creating a SplitView widget to display multiple panes in a tablet and
building interaction between the panes   157
Tab between views in the application using a TabStrip widget   163

Chapter 10: Kendo UI DataViz   167
Introduction   167
Creating charts using kendoChart   168
Binding a chart to a DataSource object   173
Creating a multiaxis chart   177
Displaying data over a period of time and using aggregate functions   181
Making a chart interactive by adding events   185
Changing the chart type dynamically   188

Chapter 11: Kendo UI DataViz – Advance Charting   193
Introduction   193
Creating a chart to show stock history   194
Using the Radial Gauge widget   199
Using the Linear Gauge widget   205
Generating barcode images using various encoding methods   207
Generating a QR code image to represent a URL, e-mail, telephone,
and geographic location   209
Creating flow diagrams using Kendo Diagram   211
Creating hierarchical structural diagrams using layouts   215
Creating a map to display geospatial information using an OpenStreet map   220
Creating a map by binding it to the GeoJSON data   225

Index   229

Preface

Kendo UI is an HTML- and jQuery-based client-side framework that enables you to build web applications for the web and mobile platforms. The library contains a multitude of widgets that can be configured with ease to build applications rapidly. In addition to the widgets for the web and mobile platforms, the library provides numerous data-visualization components that allow you to build complex charts, diagrams, interactive maps, and barcode and QR code generators.

What this book covers

Chapter 1, The Kendo UI Application Framework, introduces you to the core components in the framework, such as client-side templates, using the Model View ViewModel (MVVM) pattern, and using the built-in validator to validate form fields.

Chapter 2, The Kendo UI Grid, introduces you to the Grid component that is used to display data in a tabular format and includes various features such as sorting based on the selected column, filtering data that match certain criteria, and updating data.

Chapter 3, Kendo UI TreeView, introduces you to the TreeView widget that is used to display hierarchical data such as a directory structure. The widget can be customized by prefixing the components in TreeView with a checkbox or representing them with a prefixed image.

Chapter 4, Kendo UI Editor, introduces you to the Editor widget that allows you to create a What You See Is What You Get (WYSIWYG) interface. This interface contains a number of tools that can be added to the toolset bar.

Chapter 5, Kendo UI PanelBar, introduces you to the PanelBar component that is used to construct an accordion-like layout. This layout allows you to group data and stack them vertically.

Chapter 6, Kendo UI File Uploader, introduces you to the Upload widget that allows you to upload multiple files to the server and track the progress of the same. It provides a consistent interface for all browsers.

Chapter 7, Kendo UI Window, introduces you to the Window widget that is used to create pop-up windows or modal windows to display alert messages.

Chapter 8, Kendo UI Mobile Framework, introduces you to the mobile framework, which includes core mobile components used in building a mobile application. This also includes creating layouts and views, navigating through views, and adding touch events.

Chapter 9, Kendo UI Mobile Widgets, introduces you to the mobile widgets in the Kendo UI Mobile library. These widgets allow you to build mobile applications quickly. This includes the use of widgets such as ListView, ActionSheet, TabStrip, and SplitView for tablet applications.

Chapter 10, Kendo UI DataViz, introduces you to the basic data visualization components that allow you to create interactive charts easily. These components can also be customized to match the desired look and feel.

Chapter 11, Kendo UI DataViz – Advance Charting, introduces you to the advanced data visualization components that allow you to build dashboard-like applications with ease. This includes creating a Stock chart, creating a radial and linear gauge, generating barcode and QR code, creating flowchart-like diagrams, creating diagrams to represent a hierarchical structure, and creating maps to display geospatial data.

What you need for this book

This book includes numerous recipes on building applications using web, mobile, and data visualization components. You are required to download the Kendo UI framework from www.kendoui.com. The library has a dependency on the jQuery framework and therefore should be loaded before including the Kendo UI library.

Basic knowledge of building web applications using HTML, CSS, and JavaScript is required. It will be helpful if you have used jQuery in your projects.

Who this book is for

This book will do wonders for web developers who have knowledge of HTML and JavaScript and want to polish their skills in building applications using the Kendo UI library.

The library provides web, mobile, and data visualization widgets that can be configured easily to match the needs of the application.

Conventions

In this book, you will find a number of styles of text that distinguish between different kinds of information. Here are some examples of these styles, and an explanation of their meaning.

Code words in text, database table names, folder names, filenames, file extensions, pathnames, dummy URLs, user input, and Twitter handles are shown as follows: "The Kendo UI library exports an object, kendo, which is a namespace for various other objects and functions."

A block of code is set as follows:

```
var template = kendo.template("Full Name: " +
                        "<span> #= lastName # </span>," +

                        "<span> #= firstName # </span>");
```

When we wish to draw your attention to a particular part of a code block, the relevant lines or items are set in bold:

```
<div
   data-role="view"
   data-layout="defaultLayout">
   <div
      id="touchSurface"
      data-role="touch"
      data-enable-swipe="1"
      data-touchstart="touchstart"
      data-swipe="swipe"
      data-tap="tap"
      data-doubletap="doubletap"
      data-hold="hold"
      style="height: 200px;">

      Touch Surface

   </div>
</div>
```

Any command-line input or output is written as follows:

Directory1 is checked: no

New terms and **important words** are shown in bold. Words that you see on the screen, in menus or dialog boxes for example, appear in the text like this: "For example, if the first name is not specified, the message would be **First Name is required**."

 Warnings or important notes appear in a box like this.

 Tips and tricks appear like this.

Reader feedback

Feedback from our readers is always welcome. Let us know what you think about this book—what you liked or may have disliked. Reader feedback is important for us to develop titles that you really get the most out of.

To send us general feedback, simply send an e-mail to `feedback@packtpub.com`, and mention the book title via the subject of your message.

If there is a topic that you have expertise in and you are interested in either writing or contributing to a book, see our author guide on `www.packtpub.com/authors`.

Customer support

Now that you are the proud owner of a Packt book, we have a number of things to help you to get the most from your purchase.

Downloading the example code

You can download the example code files for all Packt books you have purchased from your account at `http://www.packtpub.com`. If you purchased this book elsewhere, you can visit `http://www.packtpub.com/support` and register to have the files e-mailed directly to you.

Errata

Although we have taken every care to ensure the accuracy of our content, mistakes do happen. If you find a mistake in one of our books—maybe a mistake in the text or the code—we would be grateful if you would report this to us. By doing so, you can save other readers from frustration and help us improve subsequent versions of this book. If you find any errata, please report them by visiting `http://www.packtpub.com/submit-errata`, selecting your book, clicking on the **errata submission form** link, and entering the details of your errata. Once your errata are verified, your submission will be accepted and the errata will be uploaded on our website, or added to any list of existing errata, under the Errata section of that title. Any existing errata can be viewed by selecting your title from `http://www.packtpub.com/support`.

Piracy

Piracy of copyright material on the Internet is an ongoing problem across all media. At Packt, we take the protection of our copyright and licenses very seriously. If you come across any illegal copies of our works, in any form, on the Internet, please provide us with the location address or website name immediately so that we can pursue a remedy.

Please contact us at copyright@packtpub.com with a link to the suspected pirated material.

We appreciate your help in protecting our authors, and our ability to bring you valuable content.

Questions

You can contact us at questions@packtpub.com if you are having a problem with any aspect of the book, and we will do our best to address it.

1
The Kendo UI Application Framework

In this chapter, we will cover the following recipes:

- Using client-side templates to generate HTML markup from JSON data
- Creating a two-way binding between `View` elements and JavaScript objects using the **Model View ViewModel** (**MVVM**) pattern
- Using `source` and `template` binding with `ViewModel` to generate HTML content
- Validating user input using the built-in Validator

Introduction

The Kendo UI library is composed of various widgets that are built for both the web and mobile platform. It also provides data visualization components, which can be used to build rich and interactive charts. This chapter focuses on the Kendo UI application framework. This framework includes tools such as the client-side templating engine, data binding, and routing, and it also helps users to validate form fields.

Using client-side templates to generate HTML markup from a JSON data

The concept of using a templating system with some data source to generate a dynamic web content has been around web development for a long time. Java Server Pages (Java), Smarty (PHP), and Django (Python) are examples of some of the server-side templating engines. Generating content at runtime used to be a server-side-only affair. In recent years, generating the content on the client side (on the browser) has been embraced.

The dynamic applications that are being built today require the user interface to be updated frequently. This can be achieved by fetching the HTML fragment from the server and then inserting it into the document. However, this requires the server to generate such fragments as opposed to delivering complete web pages. In the client-side templating engine, the servers are responsible for sending only the dynamic data in the JSON format and then have the page assembled in the browser using a static client-side template. This template can be served from **Content Delivery Network** (**CDN**) instead of the same server that sends the dynamic data. The time taken to send the records in the form of JSON data and not generate the markup on the server side takes away more CPU cycles, thereby improving the performance of the application to a great extent. Consider a shopping cart application, which lists the products in the cart. The cart data can be sent to the client in the JSON format. Then, use templates to generate an HTML markup on the client side.

There are various types of client-side templating engines to choose from; some of them are logic-less such as Mustache and Handlebars, some are based on the HAML syntax such as Jade, and some others are based on John Resig's micro templating such as `underscore.js`.

In Kendo UI, a microtemplating library is used, which is called hash templates. In these templates, hash symbols are used to mark regions in the template that will be executed when the template is used to generate dynamic content.

How to do it...

The Kendo UI library exports an object, `kendo`, which is a namespace for various other objects and functions. The template function is one of them. The template function compiles hash-based templates into functions that can be evaluated for rendering. It is useful to render complicated bits of HTML from a JSON data source. The following are the three hash-based syntaxes:

- The syntax to render literal values is `#=   #`
- The syntax to render HTML-encoded values is `#:   #`
- The syntax to execute arbitrary JavaScript code is `# for(...) #`

Let's take a look at a very simple example of rendering `firstName` and `lastName` of a person using the following hash-based template:

```
<script>

  var template = kendo.template("Full Name: " +
    "<span> #= lastName # </span>,"  +
    "<span> #= firstName # </span>");
  var data = {};

  data.lastName = "Smith";
  data.firstName = "Todd";

  var result = template(data);

  $('.addressContainer').append(result);

</script>
```

Downloading the example code

You can download the example code files for all Packt books you have purchased from your account at `http://www.packtpub.com`. If you purchased this book elsewhere, you can visit `http://www.packtpub.com/support` and register to have the files e-mailed directly to you.

Here, the `#= <literal> #` expression is used. Similarly, we can also use a hash-based expression to render HTML-encoded values:

```
<script>

  var template = kendo.template("Full Name: <span> # lastName # #
    </span>, <span> #: firstName # </span>");
  var data = {};

  data.lastName = "<b>Smith</b>";
  data.firstName = "<i>Todd</i>";

  var result = template(data);

  $('.addressContainer').append(result);

</script>
```

Here, the `#: <literal> #` expression is used. Rendering HTML-encoded values is particularly useful when you are accepting HTML strings as a part of a form input string, and they display the same in the result. The HTML characters\tags present in the data would be escaped and rendered as strings.

How it works...

Now, let's understand what is happening in the preceding code examples. In the first example, the first line is as follows:

```
var template = kendo.template("Full Name: " +
                        "<span> #= lastName # </span>,"  +

                        "<span> #= firstName # </span>");
```

Here, the template function is used to compile the input string. Note that the input string contains HTML tags with hash-based expressions. This will return a function that can then be used with data to generate output. In the following four lines of the code snippet, a JavaScript data object with two variables, `lastName` and `firstName`, is created:

```
var data = {};

data.lastName = "Smith";
data.firstName = "Todd";

var result = template(data);
```

The last line in the preceding code snippet invokes the compiled function (assigned to the template variable), which then passes the JavaScript object as a parameter. This will replace the literal values inside the hash-based expression and generate the following output string:

```
Full Name: <span> Smith </span>, <span> Todd </span>
```

In the second example, the code is very similar, except that the `#: <literal> #` hash-based expression is used. This expression will escape the HTML tags and generate the output that contains HTML tags as it is.

There's more...

As seen in the previous examples, the HTML is passed as a string to the `kendo.template` function. An alternative to this is to define a template in a script tag:

```
<script type="text/x-kendo-template" id="testTemplate">

    # for (var i=0; i < functions.length; i++) { #
      <li> #= functions[i] # </li>
    # } #

</script>
```

Note the hash-based syntax used in the preceding code as well; it contains a JavaScript `for` statement that iterates over an array and generates list tags (`<li>` tags). Now, to compile this template, we will refer to the script tag using the `id` attribute:

```
<script>

    var templateContent = $('#testTemplate').html();

    var template = kendo.template(templateContent);

    var functions = ["concat", "indexOf", "join", "lastIndexOf",
      "pop", "push", "reverse", "shift", "slice", "sort", "splice",
      "toString", "unshift", "valueOf"];

    var result = template(functions);

    $('.listContainer').append(result);

</script>
```

Here, the template is referred using the `id` attribute, `#testTemplate`. The content of the template is retrieved using `$('#testTemplate').html()`. The content is then used with the `kendo.template` function to generate the markup. This content is then inserted into the page by appending the same inside an unordered list using `$('ul.listContainer').append(result)`.

The script tag used here to write template has its type as `text/x-kendo-template`. This is a common way to implement templating on the client side. The browser simply ignores the script tag with a type that is not recognized by it.

Creating a two-way binding between View elements and JavaScript objects using the Model View ViewModel (MVVM) pattern

There are various architectural patterns that are used in most of the applications. The three very important architectural patterns are as follows:

- **Model View Controller** (**MVC**)
- **Model View Presenter** (**MVP**)
- **Model View ViewModel** (**MVVM**)

These patterns are heavily used in structuring both the desktop and server-side applications. In recent years, these patterns have been applied to client-side applications as well. Frameworks such as AngularJS, BackboneJS, and EmberJS provide components that can be readily used to build applications that follow one of these patterns. All three patterns mentioned previously try to separate the development of the user interface from the development of the business logic.

The **Model View ViewModel** (**MVVM**) pattern is an architectural pattern, which is based on MVC and MVP. Here, the model layer represents the domain-specific data. An example application will include the bank account number, the holder's name, the balance amount, and so on. The model layer represents raw data that needs to be formatted to be consumed by `View`. The `View` layer consumes the data provided by the model and formats it as required. On the other hand, the behavior of the application or the business logic is encapsulated in a layer called `ViewModel`.

There are several frameworks, such as KnockoutJS, KnockbackJS, and Kendo UI, that implement the MVVM pattern. In Kendo UI, the MVVM pattern is at the core of the application framework. The framework provides APIs using which the various components, such as model, `ViewModel`, and data binding (that binds the markup to the `ViewModel` object) can be accomplished.

How to do it...

To illustrate how the MVVM pattern is implemented in Kendo UI, let's take a look at a very simple example in which the form elements are bound to a `ViewModel` object. The `ViewModel` object, in this case, would define the model data and also the behavior for one of the elements:

```
<form id="testView">

  Firstname: <input id="firstName"
    type="text"
```

```
    data-bind="value: fisrtName">
  <br/>

  Lastname: <input id="lastName"
    type="text"
    data-bind="value: lastName">
  <br/>

  Fullname: <input id="fullName"
    type="text"
    data-bind="value: fullName"
    readonly>
  <br/>

  <input type="submit">
</form>
```

In the previous code snippet, a form with the `id` attribute, `testview`, that contains three input elements (textboxes) is created. Note the `data-bind` attribute in each one of these input elements. The `data-bind` attribute is used to specify the binding between `View` elements and the `ViewModel` object.

Here, the first input element specifies the value of the `data-bind` attribute as `value: firstName`. This indicates that the value of the input element is bound to the `firstName` model attribute. Now let's define `ViewModel`, which encapsulates the model data and behavior:

```
var viewModel = kendo.observable({
  fisrtName: "Sagar",
  lastName: "Ganatra",
  fullName: function() {
    return this.get("fisrtName") +
           ' ' + this.get("lastName");
  }
});
```

A `ViewModel` object is created using the `Observable` interface on the `kendo` object. In this example, the `ViewModel` object contains the `firstName`, `lastName`, and `fullName` attributes. Note that while `firstName` and `lastName` are of the string type, the `fullName` attribute is a function that returns a string by concatenating `firstName` and `lastName`.

Now that we have the markup and `ViewModel`, they should be tied to each other. The `bind` method is used to bind `View` components to `ViewModel`:

```
kendo.bind($('form#testView'),viewModel);
```

The first argument to the bind function is the `View` component referred by using `$('form#testView')` and the second argument is the `ViewModel` object, `viewModel`. Once `View` and `ViewModel` are bound, any changes made to the model will update `View`, and any changes made by the user will be reflected in the model.

How it works...

When you execute the previously mentioned code snippets, the form elements with the values mentioned in the model are populated, as shown in the following screenshot:

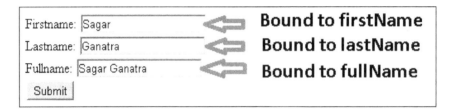

Notice that in the markup, the last input element for **FullName** is read only. It is bound to a `fullName` model attribute, which is a function that returns the string concatenated by `firstName` and `lastName`. When you change the value of either `firstName` or `lastName`, the `fullName` model also gets updated and the same is reflected in the `View` class.

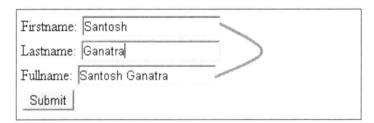

In the preceding screenshot, when the value of the **Firstname** input element is changed, the value of the **Fullname** attribute also gets updated. Note that the model attributes are updated on a blur event on the `View` component.

There's more...

In the previous screenshot, we saw how data binding can be used to set the values of input elements in the form. In addition to setting the value for some of the elements in the page, data binding can also be used to set attribute values (`attr`), to set HTML content (`html`), hide or show the elements in the page (`visible` and `invisible`), and so on.

Let's take a look at each one of these scenarios. The `attr` binding is used to bind `tag` attributes with model attributes in the following code snippet:

```
<a data-bind="attr: {href: websiteLink}"
  target="_blank">

  Click Here

</a>
```

In the preceding code snippet, the `data-bind` attribute has the `attr: {href: websiteLink}` value. Here, `attr` indicates that the tag attributes are bound to `ViewModel`. In this example, the `href` attribute of the anchor element is bound to a model attribute, `websiteLink`. The `ViewModel` object for the same would be as shown in the following code snippet:

```
<script>

  var viewModel = kendo.observable({
    websiteLink: 'http://www.packtpub.com',
  });

  kendo.bind($('a'),viewModel);
</script>
```

In the code snippet, the `ViewModel` object contains only one attribute, `websiteLink`. The value for this model attribute is an external link, which is `http://www.packtpub.com`. When the `View` component is bound to the `ViewModel` object, the anchor element is updated, which then has an attribute, `href`, that refers to the external link mentioned in `ViewModel`.

Similarly, the components in `View` can be hidden or shown on the page by using the binding attribute, `visible`:

```
<div id="view">
  <span id="container"
        data-bind="visible: isVisible">

        Some content here....

  </span>

  <br/>

  <button id="toggleVisible"
```

```
                data-bind="click: updateVisible">

        Toggle Visible

    </button>
</div>
```

In the previous code snippet, the span element has the `data-bind` attribute set to `visible: isVisible`. Here, the value of the `isVisible` model attribute should be of the Boolean type. If the same is false, then the style attribute of the span element is set to `display: none`. Also, the button has the `data-bind` attribute set to `click: updateVisible`. Here, the button's `click` event is bound to the model attribute, `updateVisible`. The `ViewModel` object for the previous markup is shown in the following code snippet:

```
var viewModel = kendo.observable({

    isVisible: true,

    updateVisible: function() {

        this.set('isVisible', !this.get('isVisible'));

    }
});

kendo.bind($('div#view'),viewModel);
```

The initial value for `isVisible` in `ViewModel` is set to true and hence the text, `Some Content here...`, (inside the span) would be visible. When you click on the **toggleVisible** button, it toggles the `isVisible` model attribute. This will either show or hide the span element.

Using Source and Template binding with ViewModels to generate HTML content

In the previous recipe, data binding between `View` components and `ViewModel` attributes was explored. Binding can be performed not only on the value of the form elements, but also on the attributes, and also to hide or show the elements on the page. In this recipe, we will look at the source and the HTML binding in combination.

Consider a dropdown (to select an element) that you want to populate it with data (option tags). The data for these could be provided from a `ViewModel` object; use a template to generate these option tags.

How to do it...

Let's first construct a `ViewModel` object:

```
var viewModel = kendo.observable({
    optionsData: [
                    {optionValue:1, optionName: "Test1"},
                    {optionValue:2, optionName: "Test2"},
                    {optionValue:3, optionName: "Test3"}
                 ]
});
```

The `ViewModel` object here contains an `optionsData` attribute, which is a collection (array) of objects. Each object in `optionsData` contains two attributes, namely `optionValue` and `optionName`. The `optionValue` attribute will be used for the `value` attribute of the `option` tag, and `optionName` will be used for the HTML content to be shown in the dropdown. The template that contains the option tag binding is shown in the following code snippet:

```
<script id="select-template" type="text/x-kendo-template">
  <option data-bind=
    "attr: {value: optionValue}, html: optionName">

  </option>
</script>
```

Here, the template with the `id` attribute set to `select-template` contains one option tag. The option tag contains the `data-bind` attribute whose value is `attr: {value: optionValue}, html: optionName`. We already saw the attribute binding in action in the previous recipe. The other binding specified here is `html`. This binding is used to generate the HTML content for the tag. These option tags should be bound to the `ViewModel` object and be encapsulated inside a select tag.

The select tag can refer to the template (mentioned previously) and bind to the `ViewModel` object using the `source` attribute:

```
<select data-template="select-template"
  data-bind="source: optionsData">
</select>
```

Here, the select tag specifies the two attributes, namely `data-template` and `data-bind`. The value of the `data-template` attribute is the `id` attribute of the template (the script tag) that we defined earlier, that is, `select-template`. This instructs `kendo` to bind the template to the `select` tag, and the generated content would become the HTML content for this `select` tag.

The `data-bind` attribute specifies a binding source that refers to the `optionData` model attribute in `ViewModel`. Now, the only step pending is to bind `View` elements to `ViewModel`, which is attained by executing the following line of code:

```
kendo.bind($('select'),viewModel);
```

How it works...

The `select` tag specifies the source binding that refers to the `optionsData` model attribute. This will make the collection of objects available to all the tags inside it.

The `data-template` attribute that refers to the template in the page is provided with the collection of objects (`optionsData`) and the template is iterated for the number of entries in the array. In this example, the `optionsData` collection contains three objects and hence, the template is generated three times and inserted as the HTML content for the `select` tag. The generated content would look like the following code snippet:

```
<select data-template="select-template"
  data-bind="source: optionsData">

  <option data-bind=
    "attr: {value: optionValue}, html: optionName"
    value="1">
    Test1
  </option>

  <option data-bind=
    "attr: {value: optionValue}, html: optionName"
    value="2">
    Test2
  </option>

  <option data-bind=
    "attr: {value: optionValue}, html: optionName"
    value="3">
    Test3
  </option>

</select>
```

The `data-` attributes would remain as they are, and the generated content now has the `value` attribute and the HTML content. Note that the preceding code could have been accomplished by using a `for` statement in a hash-based template and then appending the generated output to the `select` tag. However, using a `data-template` attribute and source binding allows you to do this seamlessly and write more intuitive code.

This pattern can be applied in various situations. Another example includes generating list tags (`li` elements) and inserting them into an unordered or ordered list.

Validating user input using the built-in Validator

Validating user-input data is one of the common tasks in any project. A client-side validation includes checking the form-input data for the type or for the missing data. This is not to say that the server-side validation is not important. However, a client-side validation takes care of performing basic validations and shows error or validation messages before submitting the form data to a server for processing. Therefore, it provides instant feedback to the user and improves the overall user experience.

With the advent of HTML5, the input fields in a form can have types defined for it. For example, an input field that should accept only an e-mail address can be specified as `type=email`. Similarly, the input fields can have types such as URL, NUMBER, RANGE, DATE, SEARCH, and COLOR. When the user specifies incorrect data for any of these fields, the browser will show an appropriate validation message. In addition to the types, the form elements can also be marked as required by adding an additional attribute, `required`, to the input elements. However, some of the old browsers don't support HTML5 features, including the previously mentioned form validation. The Kendo UI library comes with a built-in validator that can be used to perform client-side validations.

The Kendo UI validator encourages users to use HTML5-like syntax and provides out-of-the-box support to make the form validation work on older browsers.

How to do it...

Let's take a look at an example where in one input, the text field is marked as required, and the other input field of the `email` type is also marked as required. Please note that this is very much an HTML5 syntax and the user doesn't have to alter the markup to mark the fields as required or of a different type:

```
<form id="testView">

  <label for="firstName">First Name</label>
  <input id="firstName"
    name="First Name"
    type="text"
    required
    validationMessage="Please specify First Name">

  <br>
```

```
<label for="emailId">Email Address</label>
<input id="emailId"
  name="Email Address"
  type="email"
  required
  data-required-msg="Please specify Email Address"
  data-email-msg="Email format is not correct">
<br>

<input type="submit">
</form>
```

In the preceding markup, the input fields are marked as `required` and validation messages are defined in `data-` attributes. After specifying the validation messages in the markup, the last step is to attach the `kendo` validator to the form. This is attained by executing the following code snippet:

```
$("form#testView").kendoValidator();
```

In the previous code snippet, the `form` element is marked for validation by calling the `kendoValidator` function on the same.

How it works...

In the previous markup, the `firstName` field is of the `text` type and is marked as `required` by adding the `required` attribute. Also, a `validationMessage` attribute that specifies the validation message to show when the user doesn't provide any input data is mentioned. The next input element, `emailId`, is of the `email` type and is marked as `required` as well. In this case, there are two rules that are applicable; firstly, the field is required, and secondly, the user should enter a valid e-mail address. Therefore, we need to specify two validation messages for the input field. Here, the `data-required-msg` and `data-email-msg` attributes are specified. When the user doesn't specify any value, the validation message specified in `data-required-msg` is displayed. Also, when the user specifies an invalid e-mail address, the validation message specified in `data-email-msg` is displayed.

Now, let's see this in action; when the user doesn't specify values for both the fields, then the required validation message would be shown as follows:

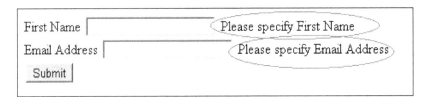

When the user clicks on the **Submit** button, the validator runs, inspects the input data, and shows the validation message if there is no data specified. Now, when the user keys in an invalid value in the e-mail field, the validation message specified in `data-email-msg` would be shown as follows:

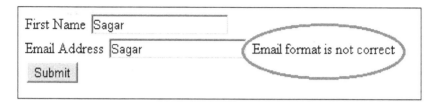

Here, both the fields have some data in place and hence, the `required` field validation has passed. However, the e-mail address is not valid and, hence, you see the corresponding validation message being shown.

> By default, the field is validated when it loses focus. This is called the `onBlur` event. This can be disabled by passing the `validateOnBlur: false` option to the `kendoValidator` method:
>
> ```
> $("form#testView").kendoValidator({
>   validateOnBlur: false
> });
> ```

There's more...

In the previous example, we saw that the validation message was specified in the markup. It is also possible to configure the validator so that the same message is applicable to all fields with a specific validation rule. For example, all required fields can have the same validation message, such as **This field is required**.

The `messages` configuration option can be used to set the various validation messages that can be applied across all the input elements, as shown in the following code snippet:

```
$("form#testView").kendoValidator({
    messages: {
    // {0} would be replaced with the input element's name
    required: '{0} is required'

    email: 'Enter a valid email address'
  }
});
```

Here, the validation messages are removed from the markup and the same is specified in the `kendoValidator` method. Note the use of {0} in the validation message for the required fields. Here {0} is replaced with the input element's name. For example, if the first name is not specified, the message would be **First Name is required**.

Similarly, in the case of fields of the `email` type, the **Enter a valid email address** validation message is shown if the user doesn't provide a valid e-mail address.

In a case where the validation message is specified in the markup as well as in the `kendoValidator` method as options, the message specified in the markup would take precedence.

It is also possible to define custom validation rules in addition to the standard set of validation rules mentioned previously. This is done by passing the `rules` option to the `kendoValidator` method. Let's consider the same example form that contains two input fields, namely `firstName` and `emailId`.

Now, let's add a custom rule that doesn't allow numbers to be entered in these fields:

```
$("form#testView").kendoValidator({

  rules: {
    customRule1: function(input) {
      var re = /^[A-Za-z]+$/;
      return re.test(input.val());
    }
  },
  messages: {
    customRule1: 'Numbers are not allowed'
  }
});
```

In the preceding code snippet, a custom rule, `customRule1`, is defined. When the form is being validated, all input fields are checked against this custom rule. Here, a regular expression is used to test whether the value of the input element contains a numeric value. If this returns `false`, then the validation message (defined under the messages object) **Numbers are not allowed** is displayed.

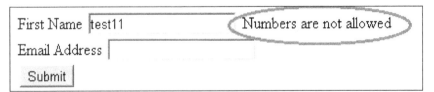

As highlighted in the preceding screenshot, the validation message is shown as the user has entered alphanumeric characters.

2
The Kendo UI Grid

In this chapter, we will cover the following recipes:

- ▸ Creating a Grid view and displaying tabular data
- ▸ Displaying data from a local or remote `DataSource` component in a Grid view
- ▸ Sorting data in a Grid using a selected column
- ▸ Using filters to display data that matches certain criteria in the Grid
- ▸ Creating, updating, and deleting content in the Grid
- ▸ Using the virtualization mechanism to improve the performance of the Grid
- ▸ Customizing the look and feel of the Grid

Introduction

The Kendo UI library comes with a powerful Grid component. A Grid component is very useful when you want to display tabular data and provide various functionalities, such as sorting based on a selected column, filtering data, using pagination, and editing the tabular data. The Kendo UI Grid component provides various configuration options to customize the way the Grid is displayed and also provides various APIs to manipulate the Grid's content.

Creating a Grid view and displaying tabular data

A Grid in Kendo UI can be created in the following two ways:

- ▸ From an existing HTML table element
- ▸ From an existing DIV element

In this recipe, we will take a look at the first approach, that is, creating a Grid using an existing HTML table element.

How to do it...

Creating a Grid using an existing table element is very easy. Let's create a table with five rows using the following code snippet:

```
<table id="grid">
  <thead>
    <tr>
      <th>Employee ID</th>
      <th>Full Name</th>
      <th>Year of Joining</th>
      <th>Designation</th>
      <th>Extension No.</th>
    </tr>
  </thead>
  <tbody>
    <tr>
      <td>10001</td>
      <td>Sagar H Ganatra</td>
      <td>2008</td>
      <td>Software Architect</td>
      <td>49523</td>
    </tr>
    <tr>
      <td>7008</td>
      <td>Adam Wayne</td>
      <td>2000</td>
      <td>Engineering Manager</td>
      <td>34890</td>
    </tr>
    <tr>
      <td>10298</td>
      <td>Nick Taylor</td>
      <td>2012</td>
      <td>Software Engineer</td>
      <td>56823</td>
    </tr>
```

```
    <tr>
      <td>10677</td>
      <td>James Thompson</td>
      <td>2010</td>
      <td>Senior Software Engineer</td>
      <td>48999</td>
    </tr>
    <tr>
      <td>6745</td>
      <td>Andrew Jones</td>
      <td>2003</td>
      <td>Senior Engineering Manager</td>
      <td>48999</td>
    </tr>
  </tbody>
</table>
```

In the preceding markup, a table element containing five rows is defined. Note that all the data is defined in the table itself. The next step is to include the style sheets in the page, which is achieved using the following code snippet:

```
<link rel="stylesheet"
  type="text/css"
  href="../../styles/kendo.common.min.css">

<link rel="stylesheet"
  type="text/css"
  href="../../styles/kendo.default.min.css">
```

The downloaded Kendo UI library contains a `styles` directory. This directory contains various style sheets. For this example, include `kendo.common.min.css` and `kendo.default.min.css`. The last step is to initialize the Grid:

```
<script>
  $('document').ready(function(){
    $("#grid").kendoGrid();
  });
</script>
```

Here, the table element with the `grid` ID is initialized by invoking the `kendoGrid` function on it. This function takes additional parameters, which are used to configure the Grid. We will take a look at these parameters in the coming recipes.

How it works...

When you render the page, you will see the previously mentioned table data being displayed inside a Grid, as shown in the following screenshot:

Employee ID	Full Name	Year of Joining	Designation	Extension No.
10001	Sagar H Ganatra	2008	Software Architect	49523
7008	Adam Wayne	2000	Engineering Manager	34890
10298	Nick Taylor	2012	Software Engineer	56823
10677	James Thompson	2010	Senior Software Engineer	48999
6745	Andrew Jones	2003	Senior Engineering Manager	48999

As seen in the previous screenshot, the columns are automatically adjusted, and each column has the same width. The previously mentioned Grid occupies the entire viewport width, unless it is wrapped inside a container with a fixed width. The column size can be changed by using the `colgroup` tag:

```
<table id="grid">
  <colgroup>
    <col style="width:130px"/>
    <col />
    <col style="width:130px" />
    <col />
    <col style="width:130px" />
  </colgroup>
  <thead>


</table>
```

Here, the width for the `Employee ID`, `Year of Joining`, and `Extension No` columns is specified as `130px`. Now, when Grid is initialized, these columns will have the specified width, and the two other columns, namely `Full Name` and `Designation`, will share the remaining space. The updated Grid is shown as follows:

Employee ID	Full Name	Year of Joining	Designation	Extension No.
10001	Sagar H Ganatra	2008	Software Architect	49523
7008	Adam Wayne	2000	Engineering Manager	34890
10298	Nick Taylor	2012	Software Engineer	56823
10677	James Thompson	2010	Senior Software Engineer	48999
6745	Andrew Jones	2003	Senior Engineering Manager	48999

As mentioned previously, the second and fourth columns in the Grid have the same width.

There's more...

Note the look and feel applied to the Grid. Alternate rows in the Grid have different colors; even the Grid header has a color applied to it. This is because of the inclusion of the `kendo. default.min.css` style sheet. The library comes with several themes, which you can apply by removing the reference to the default style sheet and then adding the reference to one of the themes. For example, the library comes with the `moonlight` theme. By adding a reference to `kendo.moonlight.min.css`, the look and feel of the Grid will change.

Employee ID	Full Name	Year of Joining	Designation	Extension No.
10001	Sagar H Ganatra	2008	Software Architect	49523
7008	Adam Wayne	2000	Engineering Manager	34890
10298	Nick Taylor	2012	Software Engineer	56823
10677	James Thompson	2010	Senior Software Engineer	48999
6745	Andrew Jones	2003	Senior Engineering Manager	48999

There are several other themes that come with the library. It is also possible to create your own theme; please refer to the following link for the same:

`http://demos.kendoui.com/themebuilder/web.html`

Displaying data from a local or remote DataSource component in a Grid view

A Grid component can be created using the data present in the page or by referring to model data, that is, data in the JSON format. The Kendo UI library provides a `DataSource` component that can be used to store a model data. The `DataSource` component can be bound to a local data source or to a remote service that returns data in either the XML or JSON format.

How to do it...

As mentioned in the previous recipe, we can either use a `table` element or a `div` element to construct a Grid:

```
<div id="grid">

</div>
```

Now, when we initialize the Grid using the `kendoGrid` function, we need to specify the configuration and data for the table:

```
$("#grid").kendoGrid({
  columns: [
    {
      field : 'movieName',
      title : 'Movie'
    },
    {
      field : 'year',
      title : 'Year'
    },
    {
      field : 'rating',
      title : 'Rating'
    }
  ],
  dataSource: [
    {
      movieName : 'The Shawshank Redemption',
      year      : 1994,
      rating    : 9.2
    },
```

```
      {
        movieName : 'The Godfather',
        year      : 1972,
        rating    : 9.2
      },
      {
        movieName : 'The Godfather - Part 2',
        year      : 1974,
        rating    : 9.0
      },
      {
        movieName : 'Pulp Fiction',
        year      : 1994,
        rating    : 8.9
      },
      {
        movieName : 'The Good, the Bad and the Ugly',
        year      : 1966,
        rating    : 8.9
      }
    ]
  });
```

In the preceding code snippet, the Grid is being initialized with two objects, namely `columns` and `dataSource`. The `columns` object is a collection of JavaScript objects that specify the column configuration. The configuration contains two properties, `field` and `title`. The `field` property refers to the field in `dataSource` that the column is bound to and `title` specifies the text to be displayed as a header in the Grid.

The `dataSource` object is also a collection of JavaScript objects that contains the data that will be displayed in the Grid. In this example, there are five objects and hence, the Grid will contain five rows.

Please note, the `columns` object can be an array of strings as well:

```
columns: ['movieName', 'year', 'rating']
```

In this case, the entries in the columns array should match the field name in the `dataSource` object. The title for the columns will be the same as the field names.

How it works...

As mentioned previously, we chose a `div` element to create a Grid. This element would serve as a container for the Grid. While initializing the Grid, the framework would look at the provided configuration and generate the markup, which will then be inserted inside the `div` element. It creates two div elements—one for the header and the other for the content. The header is shown as follows:

```html
<div class="k-grid-header" style="padding-right: 16px;">
  <div class="k-grid-header-wrap">
    <table role="grid">
      <colgroup>
        <col>
        <col>
        <col>
      </colgroup>
      <thead>
        <tr>
          <th role="columnheader"
          data-field="movieName"
          data-title="Movie"
          class="k-header">
          Movie
        </th>
        <th role="columnheader"
          data-field="year"
          data-title="Year"
          class="k-header">
          Year
        </th>
        <th role="columnheader"
          data-field="rating"
          data-title="Rating"
          class="k-header">
          Rating
        </th>
      </tr>
      </thead>
    </table>
  </div>
</div>
```

Based on the configuration provided in the `columns` object, a table that contains the header columns is generated (the `thead` and `th` tags). To display the Grid data, the library inserts another `div` element:

```
<div class="k-grid-content">
  <table role="grid">
    <colgroup>
      <col>
      <col>
      <col>
    </colgroup>
  <tbody>
    <tr data-uid="d71ac3fd-9769-4161-9277-432f151490c3"
      role="row">
      <td role="gridcell">
      The Shawshank Redemption</td>
      <td role="gridcell">1994</td>
      <td role="gridcell">9.2</td>
    </tr>
    <tr class="k-alt"
      data-uid="3240f52d-f4bb-4a2c-9985-b6ce44d75be6"
      role="row">
      <td role="gridcell">The Godfather</td>
      <td role="gridcell">1972</td>
      <td role="gridcell">9.2</td>
    </tr>
      .
      .
      .
  </tbody>
  </table>
</div>
```

The preceding code contains a table with rows that display data from the `dataSource` object. Now, when you view the Grid on the page, it will be the same as the Grid that was explained in the previous recipe. This is shown in the following screenshot:

Movie	Year	Rating
The Shawshank Redemption	1994	9.2
The Godfather	1972	9.2
The Godfather - Part 2	1974	9
Pulp Fiction	1994	8.9
The Good, the Bad and the Ugly	1966	8.9

There's more...

The `dataSource` object in this example contained the local data, that is, the data for the Grid was mentioned right within the JavaScript object. However, in most of the scenarios, the data will be fetched from a remote service. The `dataSource` object can be used to fetch data from a remote service by specifying the URL for it:

```javascript
$("#grid").kendoGrid({
  columns: [
    {
      field : 'movieName',
      title : 'Movie'
    },
    {
      field : 'year',
      title : 'Year'
    },
    {
      field : 'rating',
      title : 'Rating'
    }
  ],
  dataSource: {
    transport: {
      read: 'http://localhost/kendo/code/chapter2/remote.json'
    }
  }
});
```

In the preceding code snippet, the `DataSource` object has changed. It now contains a reference to the URL of a remote service (under the `transport` option). When the Grid is initialized, a `GET` request to the specified URL is sent and the data received as a response is then used to populate the content of the Grid.

Sorting data in a Grid using a selected column

The Kendo UI Grid comes with several features, such as sorting by selected columns, pagination, grouping, and scrolling. These configuration options can be specified at the Grid configuration level and at the column level as well.

How to do it...

To enable the sort by column feature, set the `sortable` configuration option to `true`. This will make all the columns in the Grid available for sorting. If you want some of the columns in the Grid to not be available for sorting, then you can add the same property, `sortable`, with a `false` value at the column level as well:

```
$("#grid").kendoGrid({
  columns: [
    {
      field : 'movieName',
      title : 'Movie',
      sortable: false,
    },
    {
      field : 'year',
      title : 'Year'
    },
    {
      field : 'rating',
      title : 'Rating'
    }
  ],
  dataSource: {
    transport: {
      read: 'http://localhost/kendo/code/chapter2/remote.json'
    }
  },
  sortable: true
});
```

Here, by adding `sortable` as `true`, all the columns in the Grid will be available for sorting. At the column level, for the `movieName` field, the `sortable` option is set to `false`. This will disable the sorting functionality on the first column. Also, note that adding the `sortable` option for each column is not required since this is specified at the Grid level.

In many scenarios, you would like the Grid columns to be sorted by multiple columns. In our example, the Grid can be sorted by `year` first and then by `rating`. To make this option available, set the option `mode` as `multiple`:

```
sortable: {
  mode: 'multiple'
}
```

By default, the value for `mode` is `single`, that is, the columns will be sorted based on the selected column.

How it works...

When you render the Grid with the `sortable` mode set to either `single` or `multiple`, the Grid is shown as it is. However, when you hover over a `sortable` column, the cursor changes to a pointer and when you click on it, the Grid gets sorted by the selected column. In the `single` mode, the Grid is sorted based on the selected column, as shown in the following screenshot:

Movie	Year	Rating ▲
Pulp Fiction	1994	8.9
The Good, the Bad and the Ugly	1966	8.9
The Godfather - Part 2	1974	9
The Shawshank Redemption	1994	9.2
The Godfather	1972	9.2

Here, the Grid is sorted by the third column, `Rating`; an upward arrow indicates that the Grid is sorted in the ascending order. Based on this column, the data in the Grid is sorted.

Now, let's take a look at an example where the `sortable` mode is set to `multiple`. As mentioned earlier, this mode allows users to sort by multiple columns. This example allows the columns in the Grid to be sorted by the first selected column and then by the second selected column.

Movie	Year ▼	Rating ▼
The Shawshank Redemption	1994	9.2
Pulp Fiction	1994	8.9
The Godfather - Part 2	1974	9
The Godfather	1972	9.2
The Good, the Bad and the Ugly	1966	8.9

Here, the Grid is sorted by the second column, `Year`, first and then by the third column, `Rating`. A downward arrow indicates that the column is sorted in the descending order. Here, the Grid is sorted by listing the recent movies that have high ratings.

Using filters to display data that matches certain criteria in the Grid

Similar to sorting columns in a Grid, you can update the Grid content by applying a filter. By applying a filter on the column, users will be able to search relevant data in the Grid that matches some criteria.

How to do it...

To make the columns in the Grid filterable, set the configuration option, `filterable`, to `true`, as shown in the following line of code. Similar to the `sortable` option, all columns in the Grid will be available for filtering by default. If you want some of the columns to not be available for filtering, then set `filterable` as `false` under columns.

```
filterable: true
```

How it works...

When you mark the columns for filtering, you will see a **filter** icon for each of the columns in the Grid.

Movie	Year	Rating
The Shawshank Redemption	1994	9.2
The Godfather	1972	9.2
The Godfather - Part 2	1974	9
Pulp Fiction	1994	8.9
The Good, the Bad and the Ugly	1966	8.9

When you click on it, you will be presented with a set of options that will allow you to get filtered data.

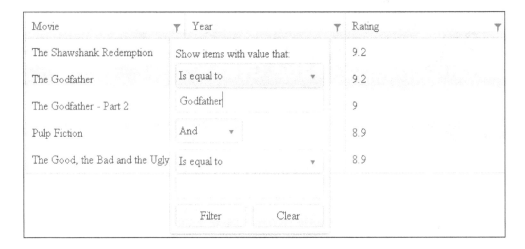

By default, users will be presented with two conditions to enter in the search criteria. In this example, the user has selected **contain** from the dropdown and specified the **Godfather** text. On clicking on the **Filter** button, the Grid will be updated to show those movies that contain the name **Godfather**. In this example, two rows will be shown, as shown in the following screenshot:

After applying the filter, you will see that the Grid gets updated and lists only two rows. The column's **filter** icon now has a white background, which indicates that a filter has been applied on the column. To clear the filter, click on the same **filter** icon and select the **Clear** option. This will clear the filter and show the entire Grid. When applying a filter, apart from specifying the **contains** condition, a user will have options to specify it as **Is equal to**, **Is not equal to**, **Starts with**, **Does not contain**, and **Ends with**.

Now, when you try to apply a filter on the second column, that is, `Year`, you will see that the Grid will not get updated and will throw the **Uncaught TypeError: Object 1994 has no method 'toLowerCase** error in the console. The library assumes that all columns in the Grid are of the `string` type and hence the error.

To get around this, define a schema in the `DataSource` object, as shown in the following code snippet:

```
dataSource: {
  transport: {
    read: 'http://localhost/kendo/code/chapter2/remote.json'
  },

  schema: {
    model: {
      fields: {
        movieName: { type: "string" },
        year: { type: "number" },
        rating: { type: "number" }
      }
    }
  }
}
```

This will instruct the framework to use the correct data type when applying the filter on columns.

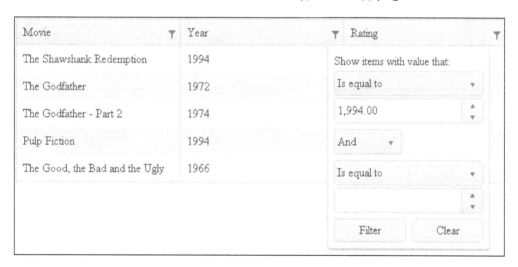

Here, the framework sees that the `Year` field is of `number` type and shows the filter criteria with different conditions in the dropdown. The list contains the **Is equal to**, **Is not equal to**, **Is greater than**, **Is greater than or equal to**, **Is less than**, and **Is less than or equal to** conditions.

There's more...

In the previous example, when you click on the **filter** icon on a column, you will see two criterias being shown. Along with this, you can specify the logical operation (AND or OR) to be performed. More often than not, you would like only one criterion to be specified. The filter criteria can be configured to show only one criterion by setting the `extra` configuration option to `false`:

```
filterable: {
  extra: false
}
```

Now, only one dropdown that lists the criteria will be shown, as displayed in the following screenshot:

Also, note that the search criteria has various operators, as mentioned earlier. The set of operators can be configured by specifying this in the `filterable` configuration, as shown in the following code snippet:

```
filterable: {
  extra: false,
  operators: {
    number: {
      eq : 'Is equal to',
      neq: 'Is not equal to'
    }
  }
}
```

Here, the `operators` object specifies the set of operators to be displayed for each datatype. In this case, for the `number` datatype, the set of operators include **Is equal to** and **Is not equal to**, as shown in the following screenshot:

Movie	Year	Rating
The Shawshank Redemption	1994	Show items with value that:
The Godfather	1972	Is equal to
The Godfather - Part 2	1974	Is equal to
Pulp Fiction	1994	Is not equal to
The Good, the Bad and the Ugly	1966	8.9

Creating, updating, and deleting in Grid

Editing the records right within the Grid is another common task. The Kendo UI Grid allows users to edit the content in the Grid, which is similar to editing the cells in an Excel sheet. There are two modes, `inline` and `popup`, in which a single row in a Grid can be edited. The `inline` editing turns the cell into a text-input field and provides options to update the record. In the `popup` editing, a pop up that contains the same fields is shown, and it allows users to save the selected record.

In addition to editing rows in the Grid, the library also allows you to delete and add records to the Grid. These actions—`Create`, `Read`, `Update`, and `Delete`—are mapped to a remote service that can process these requests. A common paradigm used in web development is to provide a RESTful web service. A RESTful service provides a single endpoint URL and provides resources that get invoked based on the `http` method mentioned in the request.

How to do it...

To enable editing of rows in a Grid, set the `editable` attribute to either `inline` or `popup`:

```
editable: 'inline'
```

This will enable the `inline` editing. The next step is to add **Edit** and **Delete** action buttons for each row. In the `columns` configuration, you can define commands that can be applied to each row in the Grid. There are two built-in commands, namely `edit` and `delete`.

The `edit` command enables the editing of the row by turning the fields in the row to input fields. The `delete` command, on the other hand, deletes the selected row using the following code snippet:

```
columns: [{
    field : 'movieName',
    title : 'Movie',
  }, {
```

```
      field : 'year',
      title : 'Year'
    },{
      field : 'rating',
      title : 'Rating'
    },{
      command: ['edit', 'destroy']
    }
  ]
```

Here, the `columns` configuration lists the various fields and mentions the `edit` and `destroy` commands. This will add the **Edit** and **Delete** buttons for each row in the Grid. These buttons should be bound to a remote service so that when the user updates or deletes a record, the service will update the same in the database. In earlier recipes, we looked at using the `DataSource` object with a `transport` attribute. Here, you can use the same attribute to specify the endpoint for each of the actions, as shown in the following code snippet:

```
dataSource: {
  transport: {
    read: '/test',
    create: {
      url: '/test',
      type: 'POST'
    },
    update: {
      url: '/test',
      type: 'PUT'
    },
    destroy: {
      url: '/test',
      type: 'DELETE'
    }
  },

  schema: {
    model: {
      id: "movieName",
      fields: {
        movieName: { type: "string" },
        year: { type: "number" },
        rating: { type: "number" }
      }
    }
  }
}
```

In the preceding code snippet, the transport object defines endpoint URLs for various actions, such as `read`, `create`, `update`, and `delete`. The `create`, `update`, and `delete` actions specify the endpoint URL as well as the `http` method to use when sending a request. The `http` method is required if you have a RESTful service that accepts the request and invokes the correct resource by examining the `http` method in the request. If this is not specified, then a `GET` request is sent by default.

How it works...

After setting the `editable` attribute to `inline` and adding its command configuration in columns, each row in the Grid has two buttons, that is, **Edit** and **Delete**, as shown in the following screenshot:

Movie	Year	Rating		
The Shawshank Redemption	1994	9.2	✎ Edit	✕ Delete
The Godfather	1972	9.2	✎ Edit	✕ Delete
The Godfather - Part 2	1974	9	✎ Edit	✕ Delete
Pulp Fiction	1994	8.9	✎ Edit	✕ Delete
The Good, the Bad and the Ugly	1966	8.9	✎ Edit	✕ Delete

When you click on **Edit**, the selected row switches to the edit mode and text-input fields are shown.

Movie	Year	Rating		
The Shawshank Redemption	1994	9.2	✎ Edit	✕ Delete
The Godfather	1972	9.2	✎ Edit	✕ Delete
The Godfather - Part 2	1,974.00	9.00	✓ Update	⊘ Cancel
Pulp Fiction	1994	8.9	✎ Edit	✕ Delete
The Good, the Bad and the Ugly	1966	8.9	✎ Edit	✕ Delete

After changing the values and clicking on **Update**, a PUT request is sent to the mentioned URL with the model data in the request body. Here, the user also has an option to cancel the operation. Similarly, when you click on the **Delete** button, an alert box asking the user to confirm the delete operation is shown. If the user clicks on **OK**, then a DELETE request is sent to the mentioned service and the corresponding row in the Grid is deleted. When you change the editable attribute to popup, a pop-up window is shown when you click on the **Edit** button.

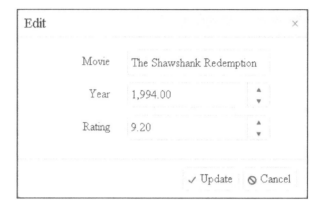

There's more...

The Kendo UI Grid also allows the user to add records to the Grid. The Grid component can define a toolbar attribute whose value is an array that contains a set of action buttons to be shown. In this case, to add new records to the Grid, specify the value as create:

```
toolbar: ['create']
```

This will add a **Add new record** button at the top of the Grid, as shown in the following screenshot:

On clicking on the **Add new record** button, a row is added to the Grid.

+ Add new record				
Movie	Year	Rating		
	0.00	0.00	✓ Update	⊘ Cancel
The Shawshank Redemption	1994	9.2	✎ Edit	× Delete
The Godfather	1972	9.2	✎ Edit	× Delete
The Godfather - Part 2	1974	9	✎ Edit	× Delete
Pulp Fiction	1994	8.9	✎ Edit	× Delete
The Good, the Bad and the Ugly	1966	8.9	✎ Edit	× Delete

This is the case when the `editable` attribute is set to `inline`. If the same is set to `popup`, then a pop-up window is shown. After clicking on **Update**, a `POST` request (refer to `create` in `transport`, shown in the last example in the *How to do it...* section) is sent to the service, mentioning the model data in the request body.

Using the virtualization mechanism to improve the performance of the Grid

Consider a scenario wherein the service returns a large dataset that needs to be displayed in the Grid. For example, say the dataset has about 10,000 records. As explained earlier, a table row is created for each record in the `DataSource` object. In this case, there are 10,000 records, and creating a table row (`tr`) for each record would make the browser run out of memory. Creating 10,000 DOM nodes and then appending the same into the document tree would consume a lot of memory. One way to tackle this problem is to use virtualization. In virtualization, only a fixed set of nodes are created and when the user scrolls over the Grid, the existing nodes are updated to show the next set of records in `DataSource`. This way, we not only optimize the use of the browser memory by reusing the DOM node, but we also provide a smooth experience to the user while scrolling through a massive list.

How to do it...

The first step to virtualization is to set the number of table rows to be displayed. These table rows will be reused to display the large list of records in the DataSource object. Let's first set the pageSize attribute in the DataSource object to the number of rows that you want to show using the following code snippet:

```
dataSource: {
  transport: {
    read: 'http://localhost/kendo/code/chapter2/remote.json',
  },

  pageSize: 4,
}
```

The next step is to specify the scrollable object with the virtual attribute set to true:

```
scrollable: {
  virtual: true
}
```

By setting the virtual attribute to true, the virtualization of data will be enabled.

 The value 4 set for the pageSize attribute is for demonstration purposes only. You should be setting this to a larger value depending on the number of records and the one that best matches the user experience.

How it works...

When you set the pageSize attribute to 4 and virtual to true, only four rows will be displayed and only four nodes are created, as shown in the following screenshot:

Movie	Year	Rating
The Shawshank Redemption	1994	9.2
The Godfather	1972	9.2
The Godfather - Part 2	1974	9
Pulp Fiction	1994	8.9

The previous screenshot shows you the Grid with four rows and a scrollbar. When you scroll, the same DOM nodes will be reused, that is, only the content and attributes of the DOM nodes are updated with the new data present in the `DataSource` object. Let's examine the DOM tree when the Grid is rendered, as shown in the following screenshot:

```
▼ <tbody>
  ▶ <tr data-uid="bbcea6f3-5e2a-4879-9a72-65a6a716a40a" role="row">…</tr>
  ▶ <tr class="k-alt" data-uid="f3b539d9-431a-4808-92a7-029858b6ca5a" role="row">…</tr>
  ▶ <tr data-uid="1e87edde-e2af-4407-adba-0aa9fdb3d485" role="row">…</tr>
  ▶ <tr class="k-alt" data-uid="296d489d-8018-4155-85ef-eb0c1c19b4f9" role="row">…</tr>
  </tbody>
```

Now, when you scroll, the same DOM nodes are reused.

```
▼ <tbody>
  ▶ <tr data-uid="f3b539d9-431a-4808-92a7-029858b6ca5a" role="row">…</tr>
  ▶ <tr class="k-alt" data-uid="1e87edde-e2af-4407-adba-0aa9fdb3d485" role="row">…</tr>
  ▶ <tr data-uid="296d489d-8018-4155-85ef-eb0c1c19b4f9" role="row">…</tr>
  ▶ <tr class="k-alt" data-uid="ccea6e15-8af8-47dd-a106-4ce4f7060666" role="row">…</tr>
  </tbody>
```

Note the `data-uid` attribute of the DOM nodes in the two screenshots shown earlier. When you scroll, the DOM nodes are transferred up by one level, and the last node that contains the fifth element in `DataSource` is referred as the fourth row in the table (since `pageSize` is four).

There's more...

When working with remote data sources, only a set of records are fetched. When the user scrolls down, the next sets of records are fetched from a remote service. In this case, operations such as sorting or filtering cannot be performed at the client side. This is because the browser can only operate on the data it has received from the service. These operations have to be performed at the server side. To enable them, set the `serverSorting` and `serverFiltering` attributes to `true` in the `DataSource` object, as shown in the following code snippet:

```
dataSource: {
  transport: {
    read: 'http://yourdomain.com/serviceName',
  },

  pageSize: 4,

  serverSorting: true,
  serverFiltering: true
}
```

Now, when you click on the column header, the records are sorted at the server side and the Grid is updated to show you the list of records sorted by the selected column.

Customizing the look and feel of the Grid

In this recipe, we will look at how we can customize the look and feel of the rows by using a template. We will also look at the reordering and resizing of columns in the Grid.

How to do it...

Each record in the `DataSource` object will be represented by a table row (the `tr` element) in the Grid. These rows can be customized by providing a template to the `rowTemplate` and `altRowTemplate` attributes. The `rowTemplate` and `altRowTemplate` attributes are used to style the rows in the Grid. Let's first define these templates. The following code snippet is the template for `rowTemplate`:

```
<script id="gridRowTemplate" type="text/x-kendo-tmpl">
  <tr>
    <td class="details">
      <span class="movieName"><h3>#: movieName #</h3></span>
      <span class="rating">Rating : #: rating#</span>
    </td>
    <td class="year">
      <h3>#: year #</h3>
    </td>
  </tr>
</script>
```

The following code snippet is the template for `altRowTemplate`:

```
<script id="gridAltRowTemplate" type="text/x-kendo-tmpl">
  <tr class="k-alt">
    <td class="details">
      <span class="movieName"><h3>#: movieName #</h3></span>
      <span class="rating">Rating : #: rating#</span>
    </td>
    <td class="year">
      <h3>#: year #</h3>
    </td>
  </tr>
</script>
```

The only difference between the two templates is the use of the `k-alt` class in `altRowTemplate`. Notice that the first column (`td class='details'`) contains the `movieName` field as well as the rating. The next step is to specify these templates while initializing the Grid:

```
rowTemplate:kendo.template($('#gridRowTemplate').html()),
```

```
altRowTemplate:kendo.template($('#gridAltRowTemplate').html())
```

The compiled templates are assigned to the `rowTemplate` and `altRowTemplate` attributes.

How it works...

When you render the Grid, you will see that the first column contains `movieName` as well as the `rating` fields, as shown in the following screenshot:

Movie	Year
The Shawshank Redemption Rating : 9.2	1994
The Godfather Rating : 9.2	1972
The Godfather - Part 2 Rating : 9	1974
Pulp Fiction Rating : 8.9	1994
The Good, the Bad and the Ugly Rating : 8.9	1966

Also, notice the formatting of the movie name and year. Here, instead of generating table rows using the standard template, a user-specified template is used to create these rows. The hash-based templates mentioned in the document will be used to generate table rows.

There's more...

The columns in the Grid can be resized and reordered by specifying the configuration details for these while initializing the Grid:

```
resizable: true,

reorderable: true
```

By mentioning `resizable` as `true`, the columns' width can be changed, as shown in the following screenshot:

Movie	Year	Rating
The Shawshank Redemption	1994	9.2
The Godfather	1972	9.2
The Godfather - Part 2	1974	9
Pulp Fiction	1994	8.9

The columns in the Grid can be made reorderable by mentioning this attribute when initializing the Grid.

Movie	Year	+ Rating	
The Shawshank Redemption	1994		9.2
The Godfather	1972		9.2
The Godfather - Part 2	1974		9
Pulp Fiction	1994		8.9

Here, the user is trying to reorder the last column by moving it to the second column.

3
Kendo UI TreeView

In this chapter, we will cover the following recipes:

- ▸ Using a TreeView widget to display a directory structure
- ▸ Using the drag and drop feature to move elements in TreeView
- ▸ Using checkboxes to select nodes in TreeView
- ▸ Associating icons with labels in TreeView

Introduction

The Kendo UI TreeView widget allows you to display hierarchical data in a tree-like structure. This widget allows users to expand or collapse the hierarchical data. It also allows them to perform drag-and-drop operations, allowing list items to be moved from one node to the other.

Using a TreeView widget to display a directory structure

A TreeView widget can be created by specifying the hierarchical data either in the HTML markup or by binding it to a `DataSource` object.

How to do it...

To create a TreeView, let's specify the data in the markup, as shown in the following code snippet:

```
<ul id="treeView">
  <li>
    Directory1
```

```
      <ul>
        <li>File1.txt</li>
        <li>File2.txt</li>
      </ul>
    </li>
    <li>
      Directory2
      <ul>
        <li>File3.txt</li>
        <li>File4.txt</li>
      </ul>
    </li>
    <li>
      Directory3
      <ul>
        <li>File5.txt</li>
        <li>File6.txt</li>
      </ul>
    </li>
  </ul>
```

The next step is to initialize the TreeView widget by invoking the `kendoTreeView` function on the DOM node using the following line of code:

```
$('#treeView').kendoTreeView();
```

How it works...

The TreeView widget displays the hierarchical data in a tree-like structure, as shown in the following screenshot:

```
▸ Directory1
▸ Directory2
▸ Directory3
```

Note that TreeView displays only the top-level elements. It shows you a right arrow icon before the element. On clicking on the icon, the top-level element expands to show you the next level in the hierarchical structure.

By default, none of the elements in the hierarchy are expanded initially. To expand an element when it is rendered, specify the `expanded` data attribute as true:

```
.
.
<li data-expanded="true">
  Directory2
  <ul>
    <li>File3.txt</li>
    <li>File4.txt</li>
  </ul>
</li>
.
.
```

By specifying the `data-expanded` attribute as `true`, the element would expand to show you the next-level elements in the hierarchy.

There's more...

The TreeView widget can be created by specifying the hierarchical structure in the `DataSource` object. This `DataSource` object is then bound to a view element. Let's use a `div` element, which will be bound to a `DataSource` object:

```
<div id="treeView">

</div>
```

Now, let's bind this view element to a `DataSource` object when initializing the TreeView widget:

```
$('#treeView').kendoTreeView({
  dataSource: [{
    text: "Directory1",
      items: [
```

```
          { text: "File1.txt"},
          { text: "File2.txt"}
        ],
        expanded: true
      }, {
        text: "Directory2",
        items: [
          { text: "File1.txt"},
          { text: "File2.txt"}
        ]
      }, {
        text: "Directory3",
        items: [
          { text: "File1.txt"},
          { text: "File2.txt"}
        ]
      }
    ]
  });
```

Here, the `DataSource` object is an array of objects and each object specifies the properties for a node in the TreeView widget. Each object has a `text` attribute, which specifies the label for the node in the TreeView widget. It also has an `items` collection, which specifies the subitems for the node in TreeView.

The first object in the `DataSource` collection has an `expanded` attribute set to `true` to indicate that the node would be expanded to show subitems.

Constructing a TreeView widget from a remote DataSource object

It is also possible to construct a TreeView widget by fetching the data from a remote service. The `DataSource` object can specify the URL for the remote service from where the hierarchical data would be fetched:

```
$('#treeView').kendoTreeView({

  dataSource: {

    transport: {
      read: '/services/music'
    }
  }

});
```

Here, the remote service URL, `/services/music`, should return the data that contains first-level elements in the TreeView widget. Let's assume that the service returns the following data:

```
[
  {
    "categoryId": 1,
    "categoryName": "Genre",
    "hasSubCategories": true
  },
  {
    "categoryId": 2,
    "categoryName": "Artists",
    "hasSubCategories": true
  },
  {
    "categoryId": 3,
    "categoryName": "Songs",
    "hasSubCategories": true
  },
  {
    "categoryId": 4,
    "categoryName": "Playlists",
    "hasSubCategories": true
  }
]
```

The preceding JSON response from the service returns four records and these are top-level nodes in the TreeView widget. Each object in the response contains three fields; when initializing the TreeView widget, the field that should be used to display the text should be specified:

```
$('#treeView').kendoTreeView({

  dataSource: {

    transport: {
      read: '/services/music'
    }
  },

  dataTextField: 'categoryName'

});
```

Now, when you execute the previous code, you would see the category names being displayed in the TreeView widget. Here, the `dataTextField` attribute is used to specify the field name that should be used when displaying labels in the TreeView widget.

To populate the next level of nodes in TreeView, the widget should be instructed whether the current node contains subitems or not. Notice that the response contains the `categoryId` and `hasSubCategories` fields; the `categoryId` field serves as a unique ID for each object in the response and the `hasSubCategories` field indicates whether the object contains subitems. This should be identified in the `DataSource` object and hence a schema for the same should be specified:

```javascript
$('#treeView').kendoTreeView({

  dataSource: {

    transport: {
      read: 'TreeView.json'
    },

    schema: {
      model: {
        id: 'categoryId',
        hasChildren: 'hasSubCategories'
      }
    }
  },

  dataTextField: "categoryName",

});
```

Here, the properties in the schema models, `id` and `hasChildren`, are mapped to the attributes in the response mentioned earlier. Now, TreeView shows you the list of top-level nodes and indicates that each node in the tree has children. When you click on any of the nodes in TreeView, a `GET` request is sent to remote services, specifying the `categoryId` as a query parameter. For example, when you click on the first node in the tree, a `GET` request is sent with the `categoryId` query parameter set to 1:

```
/services/music?categoryId=1
```

The service is expected to return a similar JSON response, that is, a collection of objects, each containing the `categoryId` and `hasSubCategories` attributes.

Using the drag and drop feature to move elements in TreeView

In a TreeView widget, elements in the tree can be dragged-and-dropped to various levels. This is applicable not only to child elements, but also to top-level nodes in the tree.

How to do it...

To enable the drag and drop feature, specify the `dragAndDrop` property as `true` while initializing the TreeView widget, as shown in the following code snippet:

```
$('#treeView').kendoTreeView({
  dragAndDrop: true,

  dataSource: [{
    text: "Directory1",
    items: [
      { text: "File1.txt"},
      { text: "File2.txt"}
    ],
    expanded: true
  }, {
    text: "Directory2",
    items: [
      { text: "File3.txt"},
      { text: "File4.txt"}
    ]
  }, {
    text: "Directory3",
    items: [
      { text: "File5.txt"},
      { text: "File6.txt"}
    ]
  }
 ]

});
```

Here, when the `dragAndDrop` property is set to `true`, the elements in TreeView can be moved between various levels in the tree.

As the user drags the node, various events are generated. The application can listen to these events and customize its behavior. The `drag`, `dragstart`, `dragend`, and `drop` events are the set of events for which the user can specify the event listeners.

Let's consider the `drag` event. The generated event contains meta information and includes a function to set the tooltip, that is, a tooltip is shown when the user is performing the drag operation. The event contains properties such as `sourceNode`, which refers to the element being dragged; `dropTarget`, which refers to the element that the `sourceNode` is placed over; `pageX` and `pageY`, which refer to the x and y coordinates of the mouse pointer on the screen; and `statusClass`, which indicates the status of the drag operation, that is, the node being added, inserted, or denied if the operation is not acceptable.

To set the tooltip, invoke the `setStatusClass` function on the event object. This function accepts a string as a parameter, which should be one of `k-insert-top`, `k-insert-middle`, `k-insert-bottom`, `k-add`, or `k-denied`.

The `statusClass` property can be used in the `setStatusClass` function to set the appropriate tooltip while the element is being dragged:

```
$('#treeView').kendoTreeView({
  dragAndDrop: true,

  drag: function (e) {
    e.setStatusClass('k-' + e.statusClass);
  }
});
```

Now, when the element is being dragged, the tooltip is set by invoking the `setStatusClass` function. The status of the drag operation is available in the `statusClass` property of the event object.

How it works...

After setting the `dragAndDrop` property to `true`, the elements in TreeView can be dragged-and-dropped to any level in the tree.

The previous screenshot indicates that the `File1.txt` element is being dragged and the tooltip indicates that the element will be inserted at the bottom, that is, it would be the last element under the parent node, `Directory1`. When the element is being dragged, the `statusClass` property is set to `insert-bottom` and the tooltip is set to `k-insert-bottom`.

Similarly, when the element is moved to a different node, you would notice that the tooltip changes to indicate that the dragged element (sourceNode) would be added to a node in TreeView.

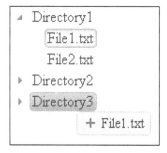

Notice the tooltip in the preceding screenshot; it indicates that the element is being added to Directory3. After dropping the element, the parent node is expanded to show its content.

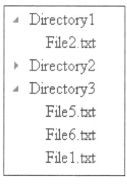

There's more...

In many scenarios, you would like one of the nodes in the tree to not accept a drop from any other element. In this case, the drop event listener can be used to prevent a drop from any node in the tree:

```
$('#treeView').kendoTreeView({
  dragAndDrop: true,

  drop: function(e) {
    if($(e.dropTarget)[0].innerText === 'Directory3') {
      e.setValid(false);
    }
  }
});
```

Here, the dropTarget node is checked to see whether it contains the Directory3 text.

If this condition is true, then the `setValid` function is invoked on the event object, passing `false` as the parameter. This will disable the drop of any `sourceNode` over the node that contains the `Directory3` text.

In another scenario, if you would like to disable the dragging of top-level nodes in the tree, that is, the root nodes of the tree, then an event listener for the `dragstart` event can be added:

```
$('#treeView').kendoTreeView({
    dragAndDrop: true,

dragstart: function (e) {
    if($(e.sourceNode).parentsUntil('.k-treeview', '.k-
        item').length === 0) {
    e.preventDefault();
    }
  }
});
```

Here, `sourceNode` is checked for parent-level nodes. If one is not found, that is, if `sourceNode` itself is the parent node, then by calling the `preventDefault` function on the event object, the action of dragging the element is disabled.

Using checkboxes to select nodes in TreeView

In TreeView, each node can have a checkbox associated with it. By using a checkbox, you can select multiple nodes in the tree and perform an action.

How to do it...

To add a checkbox next to a node in TreeView, specify the `checkboxes` attribute as `true` when initializing the TreeView widget:

```
$('#treeView').kendoTreeView({

    checkboxes: true

});
```

If you want the child nodes to be selected when the parent node is selected, then specify `checkChildren` as `true`:

```
$('#treeView').kendoTreeView({

    checkboxes: {
```

```
        checkChildren: true
    }
});
```

Now, when you select the parent node, all child nodes within the parent node would be selected. It is also possible to specify nodes as checked when they are rendered. In the `DataSource` configuration, specify `checked` as `true`:

```
$('#treeView').kendoTreeView({

  checkboxes: {
    checkChildren: true
  },

  dataSource: [{
    text: "Directory1",

    items: [
      {text: "File1.txt"},
      {text: "File2.txt"}
    ],

    checked: true
    }
    .

    .

  ]
});
```

How it works...

When you set the `checkboxes` property as `true`, you would see a checkbox before each node in TreeView.

When you check any of the parent nodes (for example, `Directory1`), the child nodes will not be selected. When you set the configuration option, `checkChildren`, to `true`, the child level nodes would be selected.

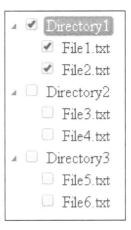

Also, note that when you select any of the child nodes, the parent node would be partially selected.

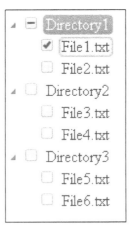

Here, the `File1.txt` child node is selected and the root node, `Directory1`, is partially selected. When you select all the child nodes, the parent node would be marked as selected.

There's more...

When you select any of the nodes in the tree, the corresponding element's `checked` attribute is set to `true`. This will trigger a `change` event on the `DataSource` object associated with TreeView. A `change` event listener can be used to check which nodes in the tree are selected:

```
var treeViewWidget = $("#treeView").data("kendoTreeView");

treeViewWidget.dataSource.bind("change", function() {
  var treeView = $("#treeView").data("kendoTreeView"),
  nodes = treeView.dataSource.view();

  (function(nodes) {
    for (var i = 0; i < nodes.length; i++) {

      console.log(nodes[i].text + ' is checked: ' +
        (nodes[i].checked ? 'yes': 'no'));

      if(nodes[i].hasChildren) {
        arguments.callee.call(this, nodes[i].children.view());
      }
    }
  })(nodes);

});
```

Here, the code checks whether the node in the tree is checked; then it iterates over its children recursively and checks whether the child nodes are checked. When you check the first node in the tree, you will see the following messages in the console:

```
Directory1 is checked: no
File1.txt is checked: no
File2.txt is checked: no
Directory2 is checked: yes
File3.txt is checked: yes
File4.txt is checked: yes
Directory3 is checked: no
File5.txt is checked: no
File6.txt is checked: no
```

Associating icons with labels in TreeView

Similar to associating a checkbox with every node in the TreeView widget, an image or an icon can be associated with a node in the tree. This icon would be displayed before the node name.

How to do it...

Let's first reference the sprite sheet and add CSS classes to the page:

```
<style type="text/css">
  #treeView .k-sprite {
    background-image:

    url('../../examples/content/web/treeview/coloricons-
      sprite.png');
  }

  .folder {
    background-position: 0 0
  }

  .pdf {
    background-position: 0 -32px;
  }

  .image {
    background-position: 0 -64px;
  }

  .html {
    background-position: 0 -48px;
  }
</style>
```

The next step would be to associate nodes in the tree with the previously mentioned CSS classes. This can be done by adding a `spriteCssClass` property for each object in the `DataSource` collection:

```
$('#treeView').kendoTreeView({

  dataSource: [{
    text: "Directory1",
```

```
            spriteCssClass: "folder",
            items: [
              { text: "File1.png", spriteCssClass: "image"},
              { text: "File2.html", spriteCssClass: "html"}
            ]
            }, {
            text: "Directory2",
            spriteCssClass: "folder",
            items: [
              { text: "File3.pdf", spriteCssClass: "pdf"},
              { text: "File4.html", spriteCssClass: "html"}
            ]
          }]

        });
```

Here, the root level nodes have the `spriteCssClass` property set to `folder` and the ones in the `items` array are set to the corresponding file type.

How it works...

When you associate the `spriteCssClass` property, the text node's `containers` (the span element) class would be set to `k-sprite` and the class name that you have specified would be the value of `spriteCssClass`. For example, the root node, `Directory1`, would have its `container` element's class set to `k-sprite folder`.

When you execute the page, you will see the icons being shown before the nodes in the tree.

4
Kendo UI Editor

In this chapter, we will cover the following recipes:

- ▶ Creating a WYSIWYG Editor using the `kendoEditor` function
- ▶ Adding and removing tools in the Editor toolset
- ▶ Using the image browser tool to insert images into the Editor

Introduction

The Kendo UI Editor widget allows you to create rich content using the **WYSIWYG** (**What-You -See-Is-What-You-Get**) interface. The interface allows you to format the text, create bulleted or numbered lists, and insert tables, hyperlinks, and images. The toolset can also be customized while initializing the Editor widget. It is also possible to create custom tools that can be used in the Editor. In addition to various Editor controls, you can use an image browser to insert images into the Editor.

Creating a WYSIWYG Editor using the kendoEditor function

An Editor can be created either by using a `textarea` or `div` element. In this recipe, we will create an Editor using a `textarea` element and show you the default tools available for formatting the data.

How to do it...

Let's first create a `textarea` element, specifying the number of rows, columns, and width:

```
<textarea id="editor"
          row="20"
          cols="80"
          style="width: 700px;">

</textarea>
```

The next step is to use this `textarea` element and create an Editor by invoking the `kendoEditor` function:

```
$("#editor").kendoEditor();
```

The `kendoEditor` function is used to initialize `textarea` as an Editor widget. The Editor will now have a WYSIWYG interface, allowing the user to format the text.

How it works...

When you initialize the `textarea` element as an Editor by invoking the `kendoEditor` function, various tools are available in the toolset, as shown in the following screenshot:

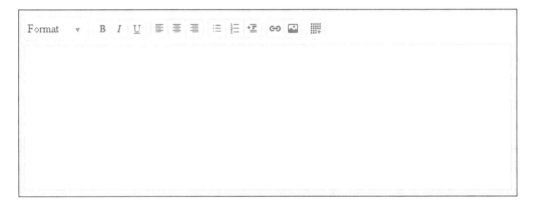

The toolset bar is shown at the top of the Editor and it allows a user to format the entered data. This includes applying different formatting for the entered text, marking the text as bold or italic, underlining the selected text, aligning the text, creating a bulleted or numbered list, and adding images and tables.

Adding and removing tools in the Editor toolset

The toolbar can be customized to include only those set of tools that are required. For example, you might like to exclude the option of inserting a table from the toolset bar, or you might like to include other options to format the text, say, changing the font color, highlighting the selected text, and so on.

How to do it...

When initializing the Editor widget, specify the tools option and include only those tools that are required to be displayed in the toolbar:

```
$("#editor").kendoEditor({
    tools: [
        "bold",
        "italic",
        "strikethrough",
        "subscript",
        "superscript",
        "foreColor",
        "backColor"
    ]
});
```

In the preceding code snippet, the tools that should be displayed in the toolbar are mentioned. These would replace the default ones.

The tools configuration option can include the Editor commands such as bold, italic, underline, strikethrough, subscript, superscript, fontName, fontSize, foreColor, backColor, justifyLeft, justifyCenter, justifyRight, justifyFull, insertUnorderedList, insertOrderedList, indent, outdent, createLink, unlink, insertImage, createTable, addColumnLeft, addColumnRight, addRowAbove, addRowBelow, deleteRow, deleteColumn, formatting, insertHtml, and viewHtml.

How it works...

As mentioned previously, when the tools configuration is specified while initializing the Editor widget, the default ones are replaced with the ones specified in the configuration, as shown in the following screenshot:

There's more...

Some of the tools, such as `fontName` and `fontSize`, list the possible values in a drop-down list. By default, a list of fonts and font sizes are listed in these dropdowns. This list can be customized in the tools configuration:

```
$("#editor").kendoEditor({
  tools: [
    {
      name: "fontName",
      items: [{
        text: "Default",
        value: "Arial, Verdana, sans-serif"
      }, {
        text: "Monospace",
        value: "monospace"
      }
    ]
  }, {
    name: "fontSize",
    items: [{
      text: "Small",
      value: "12px"
    }, {
      text: "Medium",
      value: "16px"
    }, {
      text: "Large",
```

```
      value: "20px"
    }
  ]
 }
 ]
});
```

In the preceding code snippet, the tools configuration contains an array of objects. Each object has a `name` property, which specifies the name of the tool to be used and an `items` array, which lists the values to be displayed in the dropdown. Consider the `items` array used for the `fontName` tool. It contains a collection of objects, each having two properties, namely `text` and `value`. The `text` property specifies the text to be displayed and the `value` property specifies the value to be applied when the user selects the same value from the list. In this case, if the user selects **Default** from the list then the **Arial, Verdana, sans-serif** font would be applied.

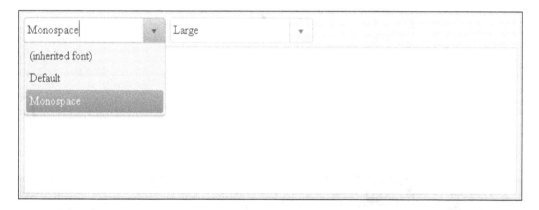

In many cases, you would like to create your own custom command that interacts with the Editor interface. For example, a custom command that would insert text into the Editor. Apart from various tools that the user can add to the toolset, the library allows you to define custom commands that interact with the Editor:

```
$("#editor").kendoEditor({
  tools: [{
    name: "custom",
    exec: function(e) {
    var editor = $(this).data('kendoEditor');
    editor.exec("inserthtml",
      {value: "Thanks,<br>Sagar Ganatra."});
    }
  }
  ]
});
```

Here, the name of the tool is `custom`, and it contains a function, `exec`. The `exec` function is executed when the user clicks on the custom tool, as shown in the following screenshot. The function first gets a reference of the Editor widget and then calls the `exec` function on the Editor instance. The function takes two parameters, namely the command name and an object that contains a set of parameters for the executed command. In the previous example, the `inserthtml` command is used to insert text in the Editor widget. The text that should be inserted is specified as a second parameter.

 The command name to be used should be one of the Editor commands.

Using the image browser tool to insert images into the Editor

One of the tools available in the Editor toolset is the image browser. The image browser tool allows you to insert an image into the Editor. It asks the user for the image URL and an optional alternate text by displaying the dialog box, as shown in the following screenshot:

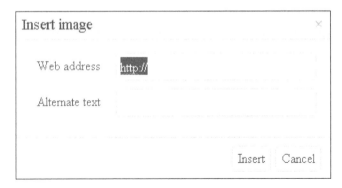

However, many of the rich applications being built today allow users to browse the images in a repository, upload images, and also remove images from the same repository. The image browser tool used in the Editor can be customized to allow these actions. In this recipe, we will see how the image browser tool is used to address such scenarios.

Getting ready

In this recipe, we will first take a look at reading images from a repository and showing thumbnails for the same in the image browser. This requires a server-side application to respond to a request that returns a JSON structure that provides metadata, such as the image name and file size.

Also, to display a set of thumbnail images, a service that returns the requested thumbnail image is required. The format of the request and fallback options are explained in this recipe.

How to do it...

As mentioned previously, we will need a service that returns a JSON structure that contains the image metadata. The format in which this data should be sent is shown in the following code snippet:

```
[
  {
    "name": "OperaHouse1.jpg",
    "type": "f",
    "size": 73289
  },

  {
    "name": "OperaHouse2.jpg",
    "type": "f",
    "size": 15289
  },
  {
    "name": "HarborBridge.jpg",
    "type": "f",
    "size": 6286
  }
]
```

Here, the structure is a collection of objects, and each object specifies the image name (the `name` attribute) and image size (the `size` attribute). The `type` attribute contains the value `f`, denoting that it represents the file type. In scenarios where we are creating a directory on the server, the `type` attribute should have the value `d`. The size of the file should be in bytes. However, when displaying the image metadata, it would be converted to kilobytes.

The next step is to specify the transport URLs to read the structure previously mentioned and to get the thumbnail images from the repository:

```
$("#editor").kendoEditor({

  tools: ['insertImage'],

  imageBrowser: {
    transport: {
      read: "/app/ImageService/Read",
      thumbnailUrl: "/app/ImageService/ThumbNailService",
      imageUrl: "/app/ImageService/Image?path={0}"
    }
  }
});
```

Here, the `imageBrowser` configuration option specifies the transport URLs to read the JSON structure that contains the metadata (the `read` attribute), the service URL that returns the thumbnail images (the `thumbnailUrl` attribute), and the service that returns the image that has to be inserted into the Editor (the `imageUrl` attribute).

How it works...

When you specify the `imageBrowser` configuration, the default dialog box is overridden and an image browser modal window is shown as follows:

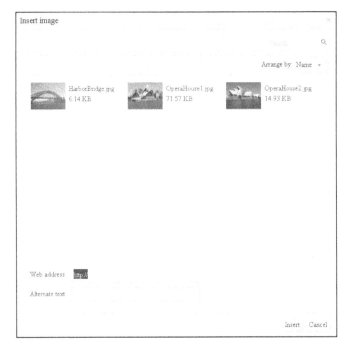

When you click on the image browser tool, first the image metadata is fetched from the URL mentioned as the value to the `read` attribute. For each object in the JSON structure, the thumbnail service is referred to get the thumbnail of the image. In our example, the image name is `HarborBridge.jpg` and the request to the thumbnail service would be `http://<domain_name>/app/ImageService/ThumbNailService?path=HarborBridge.jpg`.

Here, the query parameter, `path`, contains the name of the image for which the thumbnail has to be retrieved. Since there are three objects in the JSON structure, there would be three requests sent to the thumbnail service.

The thumbnails shown in the preceding screenshot are of the dimension 80px X 60px and show you the name of the image and its size as well. The image browser tool also has a search input field, which filters the list of thumbnails displayed in the browser. This is particularly useful if you have an exhaustive list of thumbnail images and are looking for an image by name.

On selecting the thumbnail image from the list and clicking on the **Insert** button, the corresponding image would be fetched from the service mentioned in `imageUrl`. Note the usage of `{0}` in `imageUrl`:

```
/app/ImageService/Image?path={0}
```

Here, `{0}` is replaced with the selected file name. The fetched image is then inserted into the Editor.

There's more...

The image browser tool also allows you to upload images and then insert the same into the Editor. To upload an image to the server, specify the upload service URL:

```
imageBrowser: {
  transport: {
    read: "/app/ImageService/Read",
    thumbnailUrl: "/app/ImageService/ThumbNailService",
    imageUrl: "/app/ImageService/Image?path={0}",
    uploadUrl: "/app/ImageService/Upload"
  }
}
```

Here, the `uploadUrl` attribute specifies the service that will upload the image to the server. When the `uploadUrl` attribute is specified, an **Upload** button becomes available in the image browser.

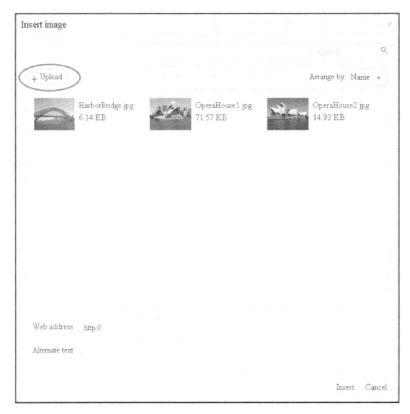

On clicking on the **Upload** button (highlighted in the preceding screenshot), the user is prompted to specify the file location. A `POST` request is sent to the service that uploads the specified image.

Once the image is uploaded to the server, the thumbnail service is queried to get the thumbnail image of the same. The upload service should ensure that the uploaded image is resized and made available in the directory where thumbnails reside.

In some scenarios, you might like to create a directory on the server and upload images there. To create a directory, specify the `create` attribute with the URL of the service that can create the directory:

```
imageBrowser: {
  transport: {
    read: "/app/ImageService/Read",
```

```
    thumbnailUrl: "/app/ImageService/ThumbNailService",
    imageUrl: "/app/ImageService/Image?path={0}",
    uploadUrl: "/app/ImageService/Upload",
    create: "/app/ImageService/Create"
  }
}
```

When you specify the `create` attribute, a button is added to the image browser screen, as shown in the following screenshot:

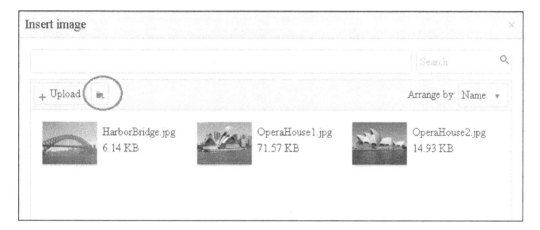

Now, when you click on the **Create** button, the image browser modal window will show you a created directory and will allow the user to specify the directory name.

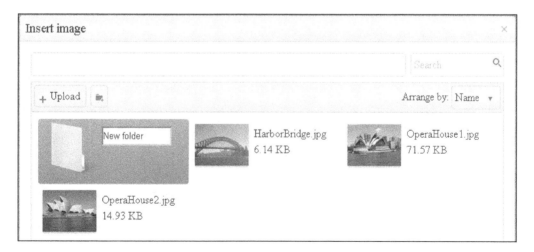

Now, the user can specify the name of the directory and hit *Enter*. This will send a POST request to the `create` service, mentioning the name of the directory in the request body (the form data):

```
{
    name: 'test',
    size: '',
    type: 'd',
    path: ''
}
```

Here, the type attribute is `'d'`, since we are creating a directory on the server. Now, the user can select the directory and upload files there. Another thing to note here is that when you are browsing through the directory, a POST request is sent to the service specified as a value to the `read` attribute. The form data contains the path details, that is, it specifies the directory name as `{'path': 'test'}`, where `test` is the directory that is to be read.

5

Kendo UI PanelBar

In this chapter, we will cover the following recipes:

- ▶ Creating a PanelBar
- ▶ Loading the content of a PanelBar using Ajax
- ▶ Binding the PanelBar to a DataSource object
- ▶ Customizing the PanelBar

Introduction

The Kendo UI PanelBar widget is similar to a tabbed panel that contains a list of items grouped under different tabs or panes. In a PanelBar, these lists of items are stacked vertically, and each list item can be expanded to show you the content. This widget is particularly useful when the data can be grouped into multiple sections and there is a constraint on the available space to display this data. For example, all your contacts can be grouped by some category such as **Favourites**, **Family**, **Friends**, and **Office Contacts**; when you tap on one of the these categories, the panel would expand to show you the list of contacts that belong to that category.

Creating a PanelBar

A PanelBar can be created either by specifying its structure in the HTML markup or by configuring it using an API. In this recipe, we will take a look at the former approach.

How to do it...

A PanelBar widget contains a list of items stacked vertically. To create a PanelBar, we will need a list of items and hence we use the HTML's ordered or unordered list. In this example, we will list travel destinations, airlines, and important sights to visit as three panels:

```
<ul id="panelBar" style="width: 400px">
    <li>
     Destinations
  </li>
    <li>
        Flights
    </li>
    <li>
        Important Sights
    </li>
</ul>
```

Here, the list contains three items and these are the headings for each panel that we want to have. Also, the `width` property is set to `400px` which will set the width of the `PanelBar` component. If the `width` property is not specified, then `PanelBar` would occupy the entire screen width, which is not desirable.

The preceding panels do not list any content yet. Let's specify the content for each of these in the HTML markup:

```
<ul id="panelBar" style="width: 400px">
  <li>
    Destinations

    <div class="destinationData">
      <h2>India</h2>
      <img src="./images/India-Flag-icon.png" />
    </div>

    <div class="destinationData">
      <h2>Australia</h2>
      <img src="./images/Australia-Flag-icon.png" />
    </div>

    <div class="destinationData">
      <h2>Indonesia</h2>
      <img src="./images/Indonesia-Flag-icon.png" />
    </div>

  </li>
```

```
     <li>
       Flights

       <div class="destinationData">
         British Airways
       </div>

       <div class="destinationData">
         Air France
       </div>

       <div class="destinationData">
         Lufthansa Airlines
       </div>

       <div class="destinationData">
         Singapore Airlines
       </div>

       <div class="destinationData">
         Qatar Airways
       </div>
     </li>
     <li>
       Important Sights

       <div class="destinationData">
         <h2>Taj Mahal</h2>
         <img src="./images/TajMahal.jpg" />
       </div>

       <div class="destinationData">
         <h2>Sydney Opera House</h2>
         <img src="./images/OperaHouse.jpg" />
       </div>

       <div class="destinationData">
         <h2>Tanah Lot Temple</h2>
         <img src="./images/TanahLot.jpg" />
       </div>

     </li>
   </ul>
```

In the preceding HTML markup, each list item contains the heading and content that needs to be displayed when the user clicks on an item in the PanelBar.

 The `destinationData` class used in the preceding code snippet is used for styling purposes only.

The final step is to initialize the PanelBar widget. To initialize, call the `kendoPanelBar` function on the list as follows:

```
$("#panelBar").kendoPanelBar();
```

How it works...

Initially, when the list contains only the headings, you will see three panes stacked vertically, as shown in the following screenshot:

When you add content to each of the items in the list, you will see a down arrow for each heading in the list, as shown in the following screenshot:

Now, when you click on one of these headings, the list item will expand to show its content, as shown in the following screenshot:

There's more...

In the preceding example, the list elements followed a single level hierarchy. The PanelBar can be customized to work with multilevel hierarchical data. The preceding example can now include important cities for each travel destination. In this case, the country name would serve as a nested panel element:

```html
<ul id="panelBar" style="width: 400px">
  <li>
    Destinations
    <ul>
      <li>
        <span>India</span>

        <div class="destinationData">
    <span>Bangalore</span>
        </div>
        <div class="destinationData">
          <span>New Delhi</span>
        </div>
        <div class="destinationData">
        <span>Mumbai</span>
        </div>
      </li>
    </ul>

    <ul>
      <li>
        <span>Australia</span>

        <div class="destinationData">
```

```
          <span>Sydney</span>
        </div>
        <div class="destinationData">
          <span>Melbourne</span>
        </div>
        <div class="destinationData">
          <span>Cairns</span>
        </div>
      </li>
    </ul>
  </li>
  <li>
    Flights



  </li>
  <li>
    Important Sights



  </li>
</ul>
```

In the preceding code snippet, the first list item contains nested list elements and each of these nested list elements contain some content, as shown in the following screenshot:

Like their parent list elements, each child list element has a heading that users can click on to expand the content.

Loading the content of a PanelBar using Ajax

In the previous recipe, we looked at how a PanelBar widget can be created using the markup present in the page. In this recipe, we will look at how the content of each list item in the PanelBar can be loaded by fetching the same from the server using Ajax.

As observed in the previous recipe, the content for each list item was wrapped inside a `div` element. By doing so, the size of the page had increased, which in turn would have affected the performance of the application. A workaround to this is to load the content of each list item when it is requested using Ajax.

How to do it...

Let's consider the same example; here, the list headings are specified in the markup and the `div` elements are used as placeholders. These placeholders will contain the data fetched from the server at runtime:

```
<ul id="panelBar" style="width: 400px">
   <li>
      Destinations
      <div></div>
   </li>
   <li>
      Flights
      <div></div>
   </li>
   <li>
      Important Sights
      <div></div>
   </li>
</ul>
```

Here, a placeholder `div` element is used so that when the PanelBar is initialized, the list headings will display a down arrow, indicating that it is expandable.

The next step is to create HTML files that would contain the content for each of the headings in the list. For example, to populate the list of `Destinations` in the preceding list, create a `PanelBar_Destinations.html` file:

```
<div class="destinationData">
   <h2>India</h2>
   <img src="./images/India-Flag-icon.png" />
```

```
    </div>

    <div class="destinationData">
      <h2>Australia</h2>
      <img src="./images/Australia-Flag-icon.png" />
    </div>

    <div class="destinationData">
      <h2>Indonesia</h2>
      <img src="./images/Indonesia-Flag-icon.png" />
    </div>
```

Similarly, pages that contain the content for the other list elements should be added.

The final step is to bind the PanelBar widget to these URLs when the same is initialized:

```
$("#panelBar").kendoPanelBar({
    contentUrls: [
        "PanelBar_Destinations.html",
        "PanelBar_Flights.html",
        "PanelBar_Sights.html"
    ]
});
```

Here, the contentUrls property specifies the URLs from where the content for each of the list items should be fetched. These are specified in the same order as list items are specified on the page.

How it works...

When the page is executed, only the list items with headings would be shown as follows:

You can inspect the DOM and see that there is no content for these list items. However, there is a down arrow that indicates that the list item contains some content.

Now, when you click on any of these list items, an Ajax request to the corresponding contentUrl is sent. The request should return the markup that should be displayed under the list item, as shown in the following screenshot:

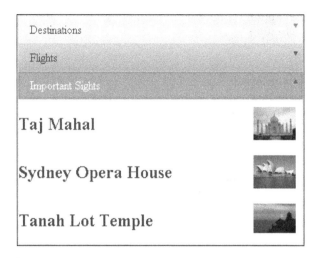

The advantage of loading the content at runtime as opposed to loading it upfront is that the size of the response from the server is reduced, and hence, the time taken to display the page is also reduced. In many scenarios where the PanelBar contains several sections, the user might not click on all of them. In these cases, it is ideal to load the content at runtime.

There's more...

When working with remote requests, there are possibilities of the server taking more time to respond, or maybe the service is not available. In these scenarios, the user should be informed of the error message or be redirected to an error page.

A series of events are generated right from when the user clicks on a list heading to the point the content is loaded in the corresponding panel. The application can specify callback handlers for these events while initializing the PanelBar widget.

Let's add event handlers to the PanelBar and log the events inside a div element (logContainer in the following code):

```
var $logContainer = $('#log');
$("#panelBar").kendoPanelBar({
  contentUrls: [
  "PanelBar_Destinations.html",
  "PanelBar_Flights.html",
  "PanelBar_Sights.html"
  ],

  select: function(event) {
```

```
    $logContainer.append($(event.item).find('> .k-link').text() + '
      selected. <br>');
    },

    expand: function(event) {
      $logContainer.append($(event.item).find('> .k-link').text() +
        ' expanded. <br>');
    },

    activate: function(event) {
      $logContainer.append($(event.item).find('> .k-link').text() +
        ' activated. <br>');
    },

    contentLoad: function(event) {
      $logContainer.append($(event.item).find('> .k-link').text() +
        ' content loaded. <br>');
    },

    error: function(event) {
      $logContainer.append('Error occurred while loading, Status: '
        + event.xhr.status);
    }
  });
```

The sequence of events is as follows:

1. When the user clicks on the list item: `select`.

2. The selected list item is expanded: `expand`.

3. When an Ajax request is sent and the content from the Ajax response
    is loaded: `contentLoad`.

4. The selected list item is activated: `activate`.

5. If there is an error in loading the content from the server, then the `error`
    callback handler is executed.

Binding the PanelBar to a DataSource object

A PanelBar can also be constructed by specifying the content in a DataSource object.
The DataSource can be local, or may refer to a remote service that returns a JSON structure.
In addition to specifying the data that needs to be displayed in the PanelBar, the DataSource
object can be used to specify some of the configuration options as well. In this recipe, we will
see how a PanelBar can be built using a DataSource object.

How to do it...

When initializing the PanelBar using the `kendoPanelBar` function, specify the `dataSource` option:

```javascript
$("#panelBar").kendoPanelBar({
  dataSource: [
    {
      text: "Destinations",
      expanded: true,
      items: [
        {
          text: "India",
          imageUrl: "./images/India-Flag-icon.png",
          cssClass: "destinationData"
        }, {
          text: "Australia",
          imageUrl: "./images/Australia-Flag-icon.png",
          cssClass: "destinationData"
        }, {
          text: "Indonesia",
          imageUrl: "./images/Indonesia-Flag-icon.png",
          cssClass: "destinationData"
        }
      ]
    }
  ]
});
```

In the preceding code snippet, the `dataSource` configuration option specifies the data that needs to be displayed in the PanelBar. The `text` attribute specifies the text to be displayed in the PanelBar header; the configuration option, `expanded`, when set to `true` will expand the panel to show you the list of items. The `items` configuration option contains a list of items that will be displayed when the panel is expanded. Each object in the `items` configuration mentions the `imageUrl` and `cssClass` properties in addition to the text that should be displayed.

In the DataSource configuration, you can also specify the URL of the page that returns the HTML content for a panel:

```javascript
dataSource: [
  .
  .
```

```
    {
      text: "Flights",
      contentUrl: "PanelBar_Flights.html"
    }
  ]
```

Here, the `contentUrl` option specifies the URL from which the content for the panel should be fetched. When the user clicks on the panel, a request is sent to the specified URL and the HTML content received as a response is then inserted into the panel.

How it works...

When you render the page, the PanelBar is populated with the data that you have specified in `DataSource`. When you check the HTML markup inserted into DOM, you will see the class specified in the `cssClass` attribute added to each list element. Also, an image is inserted inside each list element as follows:

```
<li role="menuitem" class="k-item k-state-default k-first
  destinationData">
    <span class="k-link">
        <img class="k-image" alt=""
          src="./images/India-Flag-icon.png">
    India
    </span>
</li>
```

Customizing the PanelBar

There are a few options available to customize the behavior of the PanelBar widget. In this recipe, we will take a look at setting the expanded mode for the PanelBar widget and the animation effects that can be applied.

How to do it...

The PanelBar widget is designed so that it occupies less space on the page and, at the same time, shows you the necessary content. When you click on any of the list items in the PanelBar widget, it expands to show you the content. Now, when you click on the other list item, it would also expand to show its content. At this stage, there are two items in the PanelBar whose content is being shown. By setting the `expandMode` property to `single`, only one item in the list can remain in the expanded state at any given time:

```
$("#panelBar").kendoPanelBar({
    expandMode: 'single'
});
```

By default, the value of the `expandMode` property is `multiple` and hence the behavior mentioned earlier takes place.

 In case the expanded panel contains a nested list of elements, the expanded mode won't be applied to the nested elements.

When the PanelBar is rendered, all the panels are collapsed. By adding a `k-state-active` class to one of the list items, one of the panels can be set in the expanded state:

```
<ul id="panelBar">
    <li class="k-state-active">
      Destinations
    <li>
      .
      .
    </li>
      .
      .
    </li>
  <ul>
```

The next configuration option that can be applied is the animation effects. An animation effect can be applied when you expand the panel or collapse it. Also, you can specify the duration of the animation effect as follows:

```
$("#panelBar").kendoPanelBar({
  expandMode: 'single',
  animation: {
    collapse: {
      duration: 1000,
      effects: "fadeOut"
    },

    expand: {
      duration: 1000,
      effects: "fadeIn"
    }
  }
});
```

In the preceding code snippet, the `animation` configuration is specified, which details the animation effect that should be applied when the panel is collapsed and expanded. Both `collapse` and `expand` specify the `duration` property, which specifies the duration of the animation effect in milliseconds. It also includes the `effects` property, which specifies the type of animation effect that needs to be applied. For `collapse`, only the `fadeOut` effect can be applied, whereas in `expand`, the possible values are `fadeIn` and `expandVertical`.

How it works...

When the `expandMode` attribute is set to `single`, only one panel in the PanelBar widget can be in the expanded state, as follows:

Now, when you click on the other panel, say **Flights**, then the first panel will collapse, and the selected panel will expand, as shown in the following screenshot:

6
Kendo UI File Uploader

In this chapter, we will cover the following recipes:

- ▸ Using the file uploader to upload files to the server
- ▸ Uploading files to the server asynchronously
- ▸ Listening to file upload events

Introduction

The Kendo UI library provides a file uploader widget that can be used to upload multiple files to the server. On modern browsers such as Chrome, Safari, Firefox, and Opera, the files can be uploaded asynchronously using the HTML5 File API. The enhancements to the `XmlHttpRequest` object in HTML5, such as progress tracking, are also available. On legacy browsers, it falls back and uploads the file synchronously. In this chapter, we will see the various ways in which the file uploader widget can be used to upload files to the server, showing the progress of the file upload process and the options available to customize the widget.

Using the file uploader to upload files to the server

In this recipe, we will look at how the file uploader widget can be used to upload multiple files to the server synchronously.

How to do it...

Let's create a form that will be used to upload the file as follows:

```
<form method="post"
  action="/fileUploadService"
  style="width:500px">

  <input name="files" id="fileUpload" type="file" />
  <input type="submit" value="Submit" class="k-button" />

</form>
```

The next step is to initialize the file uploader widget by invoking the `kendoUpload` function on the file input type:

```
$('#fileUpload').kendoUpload();
```

This will initialize the file input type to an uploader widget. This uploader widget can then be used to select files and upload them to the server. You can select multiple files and the same would be shown in the list.

When you click on the **Submit** button, the form is submitted to upload the files in the list. It's a `multipart/form-data` submission with the file data in the request payload. The server will be able to accept the form submission and route the user to the next page.

How it works...

When you initialize the file upload widget, you see two buttons, **Select files...** and **Submit**, as shown in the following screenshot:

 Note the look and feel of the file input type—there is a button and this is consistent across all browsers. The button allows you to select multiple files.

For the purpose of this example, let's select files twice, that is, click on the **Select files...** button twice and select a file:

Here, you would notice two files being displayed in the list. When you click on the **Submit** button, a POST request with files in the request payload are sent to the file upload service. Please note that the list also has a cross (**x**) button, which can be used to remove the files from the list.

There's more...

A few configuration options are available to customize the file uploader widget.

Disabling multiple file uploads

By default, the file uploader allows the user to upload multiple files to the server. However, in many scenarios, it is desirable to allow only one file to be uploaded. To achieve this, set the `multiple` attribute to `false` while initializing the widget:

```
$('#fileUpload').kendoUpload({
    multiple: false
});
```

This will allow only one file to be selected. When you click on the **Select files...** button again and select another file, the list will reflect the recently selected file.

Customizing the display of list items using a template

The list that is used to display the selected files can be customized by providing a template for items in the list. There are three variables available for use in the templates: `name`, `size`, and `extension`.

```
<script id="fileListTemplate" type="text/x-kendo-template">
    <div>

        <span>Name: #=name#</span>
        <span>Size: #=size# bytes</span>
        <span>Extension: #=files[0].extension#</span>

    </div>
</script>
```

Now, when initializing the file uploader, include the `template` property:

```
$('#fileUpload').kendoUpload({
        template: kendo.template($('#fileListTemplate').html())
});
```

Now, when you select files, you would see that the list contains metadata such as `name`, `size`, and `extension`.

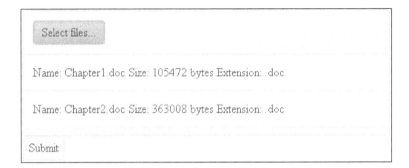

Uploading files to the server asynchronously

In this recipe, we will take a look at uploading files asynchronously to the server. This method uses the HTML5 File API to upload the files to the server. While the files are being uploaded, the progress of the file upload is shown in the uploader widget.

Getting started

This recipe will require server-side handlers that can store or remove files.

How to do it...

Let's use the same form to upload the files to the server. To upload the files asynchronously, specify the `async` configuration:

```
$('#fileUpload').kendoUpload({
  async: {
    'saveUrl': '/fileUploadService/save',
    'removeUrl': '/fileUploadService/remove',
    'autoUpload': true
  }
});
```

Here, the `async` configuration specifies the three attributes: `saveUrl`, `removeUrl`, and `autoUpload`. The `saveUrl` property specifies the service URL where the files will be uploaded. The `removeUrl` property specifies the service URL that will handle the removal of the uploaded files. The Boolean `autoUpload` property specifies whether the files will be uploaded when they are selected by the user or when the user clicks on the **Submit** button. In this example, this is set to `true`, which means that the files will be uploaded to the server when the user selects the file.

When you select multiple files using the file uploader widget, each file is uploaded asynchronously. The client sends a POST request with the file data in the request payload. It uses the `XmlHttpRequest` object to send an asynchronous POST request to `saveUrl`.

How it works...

When you select multiple files using the file uploader widget, a POST request is sent to the service mentioned in the `saveUrl` property for each selected file, as shown in the following screenshot:

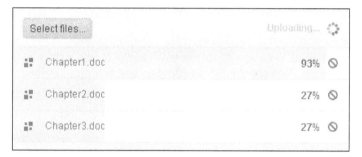

Here, three files have been selected, and each file is being uploaded asynchronously. While the files are being uploaded, the widget shows you the progress of the upload process. The file uploader widget uses the `XmlHttpRequest` object to upload the files to the server. With enhancements in the `XmlHttpRequest` object in HTML5, the file uploader widget uses the `progress` callback handler to track the progress of the file that is being uploaded.

Also, notice that the status—**Uploading** is shown in the top-right corner while the selected files are being uploaded. When all the files in the list are uploaded, the status is changed to **Done**.

Once these files are uploaded, the user can delete them by clicking on the cross (**x**) button. This will send a POST request to the service mentioned in the `removeUrl` property.

If there is an error in uploading the file, the uploader widget indicates this by marking the background color as red. It also provides you with an option to retry the file upload.

On clicking on **retry**, a POST request is sent to the URL specified in the `saveUrl` property.

When you try to remove a file from the list after the file is uploaded, a POST request is sent to the service URL mentioned in `removeUrl`. If you would like to use a different HTTP method to remove the uploaded file, then set the `removeVerb` property in the `async` configuration:

```
$('#fileUpload').kendoUpload({
  async: {
    'saveUrl': '/fileUploadService/save',
    'removeUrl': '/fileUploadService/remove',
    'autoUpload': true,
    'removeVerb': 'DELETE'
  }
});
```

Here, the `removeVerb` property is set to `DELETE`, and when the user tries to remove the file, a `DELETE` request is sent instead of a POST request.

There's more...

The file uploader widget can be localized to show a different string at various places in the widget. Also, in modern browsers, users can drag-and-drop files onto the file uploader widget.

Localizing the file uploader widget

To localize the file uploader widget, specify the localization option as follows:

```
$('#fileUpload').kendoUpload({
  async: {
    'saveUrl': '/fileUploadService/save',
    'removeUrl': '/fileUploadService/remove',
    'autoUpload': true
  },

  localization: {
    select: 'Choose files...',
    remove: 'Remove file',
    retry: 'Retry upload',
    headerStatusUploading: 'Uploading files...',
    headerStatusUploaded: 'Complete'
  }
});
```

Here, the **Select Files...** label would be replaced with **Choose files...**; the tooltip for `remove` and `retry` would be `Remove file` and `Retry upload`. While the files are being uploaded, the `Uploading files...` message would be shown and once the upload is complete the `Complete` message would be shown.

Using drag-and-drop to upload files

The file uploader widget supports dragging-and-dropping of files onto the file uploader widget. This is supported on all modern browsers that support the HTML5 File API. This method is available only if the widget has been configured to upload the files asynchronously.

When you try to drop the file(s) onto the uploader widget, it shows you the **drop files here to upload** message.

Once you drop files, the files will be added to the list and will be uploaded to the server asynchronously.

Listening to file upload events

Before the advent of HTML5, the only event listener that was available with `XmlHttpRequest` was the `readystatechange` event listener. In HTML5, several event listeners have been added to the `XmlHttpRequest` interface: loadstart, progress, load, abort, error, timeout, and loadend. In this recipe, we will see the various event listeners that can be attached to the file uploader widget and the sequence in which these events are executed.

How to do it...

The file uploader widget shows you the progress of the files being uploaded and shows the status as completed when all files have been uploaded. However, in many instances, you would like to attach listeners and listen to various events:

```
$('#fileUpload').kendoUpload({

  async: {
    'saveUrl': '/fileUploadService/save',
    'removeUrl': '/fileUploadService/remove',
    'autoUpload': true
  },

  cancel: function () {
    console.log('Cancel Event.');
  },

  complete: function () {
    console.log('Complete Event.');
  },

  error: function () {
    console.log('Error uploading file.');
  },

  progress: function (e) {
    console.log('Uploading file ' + e.percentComplete);
  },

  remove: function () {
    console.log('File removed.');
  },

  select: function () {
```

```
      console.log('File selected.');
    },

    success: function () {
      console.log('Upload successful.');
    },

    upload: function () {
      console.log('Upload started.');
    }

});
```

In the preceding code snippet, various event handlers are specified: `cancel`, `complete`, `error`, `success`, `progress`, `remove`, `select`, and `upload`.

How it works...

When you try to upload a file using the file uploader widget, various callback handlers are executed in the following sequence:

1. When you select a file or multiple files, the `select` event handler is executed.
2. When the uploader widget starts to upload the file, the `upload` event handler is executed.
3. While the file is being uploaded, the `progress` event is called continuously. Note that the event object has a `percentComplete` property, which indicates the size of the file uploaded to the server.
4. Once a file has been uploaded, the `success` handler is executed.
5. If there are multiple files being uploaded and when all selected files have been uploaded, the `complete` handler is executed.
6. If the user tries to cancel the upload while the file upload is in progress, then the `cancel` event is executed.
7. After the file upload has been completed and the user tries to remove the uploaded file from the uploader widget by clicking on the cross (**x**) icon, the `remove` handler is executed.
8. The `complete` handler is also executed when the `remove` and `cancel` events have completed their execution.

7
Kendo UI Window

In this chapter, we will cover the following recipes:

- ▶ Displaying a pop up and blocking the user interaction by configuring it as a modal window
- ▶ Customizing the look and feel of the window and including action buttons
- ▶ Using the Window API to act on a window object

Introduction

A Kendo UI Window widget is used to show any HTML content in a pop-up window or a modal window. The window content is shown on top of the other content in the page and has a title bar with a close button. The content can be either static HTML, or it can be loaded dynamically using Ajax. Any DOM node in the page can be initialized to a window, that is, the content of any element in the DOM can be wrapped inside a window. Also, the window can be resized, moved, and closed.

The Kendo UI Window widget provides several configuration options that can be used to customize the actions that can be applied and also the look and feel of the widget. In this recipe, we will first see how to create a pop-up window and configure it as a modal. Then, we will customize the look the feel of the window and use APIs to invoke actions on the `window` object.

Displaying a pop up and blocking the user interaction by configuring it as a modal window

In this recipe, we will look at how the Kendo UI window is created for a DOM node in the page. Later, we will also see how the content of the window is loaded asynchronously by specifying the URL of the page.

How to do it...

Let's create a `div` element that contains some text that will be shown in the window:

```
<div id="window">
    Window content goes here...
</div>
```

The next step is to invoke the `kendoWindow` function on the preceding DOM node:

```
$("#window").kendoWindow();
```

After initializing the DOM node using the `kendoWindow` function, you will notice that the window contains the text mentioned in the `div` element that is being shown. Note that this will not add a backdrop. To add a backdrop, the window should be configured as a modal.

The difference between a window and a modal is that a backdrop that hides the body content is shown in the case of a modal. To create the modal window, specify the `modal` property as `true`:

```
$("#window").kendoWindow({
    modal: true
});
```

By default, the value of the `modal` property is `false`, and hence the backdrop is not shown.

How it works...

When you initialize any DOM node, its content will be wrapped in a window, as shown in the following screenshot:

The window contains the **Window content goes here...** text, and the title bar has a cross(**x**) icon. If the same is initialized as a modal window, then a backdrop is added to the page, as shown in the following screenshot:

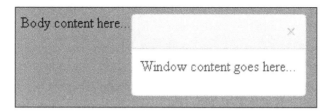

Notice that the backdrop is translucent; it shows you the text present in the page and also highlights the window. This will prevent you from interacting with the rest of the page. Usually, a modal window is used only when the user is required to complete an action before proceeding to the next step. For example, a modal window that contains a login form could be shown before the same user views the content of the page.

There's more...

The modal window can be configured to open when the user triggers an action. For example, on click of a button the modal window can be shown. Also, since the content of the modal is loaded when the user triggers an action on the page, the content of the modal can be loaded at runtime using Ajax.

Showing the modal window on a click of button

In the previously mentioned scenarios, the window or the modal window is shown when the page is loaded. In most of the scenarios, you would like to show the modal only when the user initiates an action. Let's consider that the modal window should be shown when the user clicks on a button.

Let's place a button on the page as follows:

```
<button id="btn1">Click</button>
```

To hide the modal, set the `visible` attribute to `false`, as follows:

```
$('#window').kendoWindow({
    visible: false,
    modal: true
});
```

Now, when the page loads, the modal window will be hidden. Add a `click` event handler for the button that will open the modal window:

```
$('#btn1').on('click', function() {
    var modalObject = $('#window').data('kendoWindow');
    modalObject.open();
});
```

The first line gets the instance of the modal window. Then, in the next line, the open method is called on the window instance that would open the modal window.

The `open` method is one of the several methods that can be used to act on the window object. We will take a look at other methods in the following recipe.

Loading the content of the modal using Ajax

In this recipe, the content of the modal was specified in the HTML markup. The content of the modal window can be loaded by specifying the URL that returns the HTML markup. This content will be fetched asynchronously when the page is loaded.

To load the content of the window, specify the content attribute when initializing the window using `kendoWindow`:

```
$('#window').kendoWindow({
    visible: false,
    modal: true,
    content: './jsbooks.html'
});
```

Here, the `./jsbooks.html` URL is specified in the `content` attribute. This can be any URL that returns the HTML markup. For example, it could be a PHP page that generates the HTML markup. When you load the page, an asynchronous request is sent to `./jsbooks.html`, and the generated markup is inserted into the window.

Customizing the look and feel of the window and including action buttons

There are various options available to the user to customize the window object. In this recipe, we will take a look at these options.

How to do it...

Some of the customization options for the window have a default value. For example, the pop-up window can be resized and is draggable. Also, the window is shown since the `visible` property is set to `true`. Let's take a look at some of the other properties:

```
$('#window').kendoWindow({
  visible: false,
  modal: true,
  title: "Example Modal Window",
  width: '400px',
  height: '400px',
  maxWidth: '600px',
  maxHeight: '600px',
  minWidth: '200px',
  minHeight: '200px',
  position: {
    top: '100px',
    left: '100px'
  }
});
```

Here, the `title` attribute specifies the title of the window. When the modal window is rendered, its `width` and `height` would be `400px`. This modal window can be resized; however, it can be resized to a maximum width (`maxWidth`) and height (`maxHeight`) of `600px` and a minimum width (`minWidth`) and height (`minHeight`) of `200px`. The `position` attribute specifies the `top` and `left` positions as `100px`, and the window would be positioned accordingly. If the same is not specified, then the window is positioned in relation to the document by default.

The title bar of the window can be customized to add more action buttons. By default, only the close (**x**) button is shown. The action buttons that can be added to the title bar include `Close` (added by default), `Minimize`, `Maximize`, `Refresh`, and `Pin`. These options can be specified as the value to the `actions` attribute:

```
$('#window').kendoWindow({
  visible: false,
  modal: true,
  title: "Example Modal Window",
  actions: ['Pin', 'Refresh', 'Minimize', 'Maximize', 'Close'],
  width: '400px',
  height: '300px',
  content: './jsbooks.html'
});
```

How it works...

When you execute the preceding code snippet, you will see that the window has a title bar and various action buttons, as shown in the following screenshot:

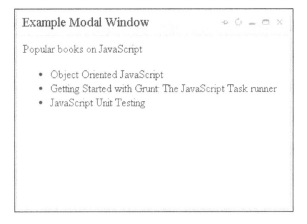

The action buttons are added in the same order as they are specified. When you click on the `Refresh` button, a request will be sent to the URL specified in the `content` attribute. If the content of the window is specified inline, that is, in the same page, then the `refresh` button is not required.

When you click on the `Minimize` or `Maximize` button, the window is adjusted such that only the title is shown or expanded to occupy the entire screen, respectively. In both scenarios, these buttons are replaced with a `Restore` button. On clicking on this button, the window is restored to its original state.

The `Pin` button allows you to fix the position of the window, that is, when the user scrolls, the window continues to be in the same fixed position. Also, if the window is pinned, the icon in the title bar is replaced with the `Unpin` button so that the user can restore the window to its original state.

There's more...

It is also possible to add a custom action button in the title bar of the window instance. Also, the action to perform when the custom button is clicked on can also be defined by adding a `click` event handler.

To add a custom action button to the title bar, first specify `Custom` in the actions array:

```
$('#window').kendoWindow({
  title: "Example Modal Window",
  actions: ['Custom', 'Pin', 'Refresh',
            'Minimize', 'Maximize', 'Close'],
  width: '400px',
  height: '300px',
  content: './jsbooks.html'
});
```

The next step is to define an event handler for the custom button added to the title bar:

```
var modalObject = $('#window').data('kendoWindow');

modalObject.wrapper.find('.k-i-custom').on('click', function() {
  alert(modalObject.options.title);
});
```

The preceding code first gets an instance of the window and then adds a `click` handler for the custom button. Here, a reference to the custom icon is used, that is, the `k-i-custom` class to add a `click` handler.

When you execute the page, you will see the custom icon being shown in the title bar.

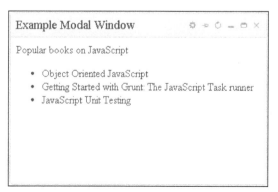

In the preceding screenshot, the first icon from the left is the custom icon. When you click on the custom icon, an alert message that displays the title of the window is shown. For a given window, you can add only one custom icon.

Using the Window API to act on a window object

In this recipe, we will look at several methods that can be used to act on the window object.

How to do it...

There are various methods available that help you act on an existing window object. These include the following methods:

- **center**: This will center the window.
- **open**: This will open the window.
- **close**: This will close the window.
- **refresh**: This will refresh the content of window. Optionally, some parameters can be passed to this function, which will override the default options.
- **maximize**: This will maximize the window to the entire viewing area.
- **minimize**: This will minimize the window to its title bar.
- **restore**: This will restore the window from its minimized or maximized state.
- **pin**: This will pin the window. It will fix the window's position, and hence, when you scroll, the window will appear at the same position.
- **unpin**: This will unpin the window and remove the fixed position.
- **toggleMaximization**: This toggles the window between the maximized and restored state.

Let's test these functions by creating a window and adding buttons that will execute the corresponding actions when clicking on them:

The following is HTML markup that contains buttons:

```
<button id="btnOpen">Open</button><br>
<button id="btnClose">Close</button><br>
<button id="btnRefresh">Refresh</button><br>
<button id="btnMaximize">Maximize</button><br>
<button id="btnToggleMaximization">Toggle Maximization</button><br>
<button id="btnMinimize">Minimize</button><br>
<button id="btnRestore">Restore</button><br>
<button id="btnPin">Pin</button><br>
<button id="btnUnpin">Unpin</button><br>
```

Now, initialize the window object as follows:

```
$('#window').kendoWindow({
    visible: true,
    title: 'Example Modal Window',
    width: '400px',
    height: '300px',
    content: './jsbooks.html',
    position: {
        top: '200px',
        left: '500px'
    }
});
```

After initializing the window, add the `onclick` event listeners as follows:

```
var modalObject = $('#window').data('kendoWindow');

$('#btnOpen').on('click', function() {
  modalObject.open();
});

$('#btnClose').on('click', function() {
  modalObject.close();
});

$('#btnRefresh').on('click', function() {
  modalObject.refresh();
});


$('#btnMaximize').on('click', function() {
  modalObject.maximize();
});

$('#btnToggleMaximization').on('click', function() {
  modalObject.toggleMaximization();

  //restore to original state after 2 seconds
  setTimeout(function () {
    modalObject.toggleMaximization()
  }, 2000);

});

$('#btnMinimize').on('click', function() {
  modalObject.minimize();
});

$('#btnRestore').on('click', function() {
```

```
    modalObject.restore();
});

$('#btnPin').on('click', function() {
    modalObject.pin();
});

$('#btnUnpin').on('click', function() {
    modalObject.unpin();
});
```

How it works...

When you initialize the window, you will see that it is positioned at 200 pixels from top and 500 pixels left of the viewport. The content of the window is loaded asynchronously since the `content` attribute that refers to the URL is specified when initializing the widget.

After initializing the widget, a reference to the window object is stored in `modalObject`. The `modalObject` is then referred to in all event listeners.

When you click on the **Refresh** button, you will notice that an asynchronous request is sent to the same URL specified in the `content` attribute. Notice that the window itself does not have the action buttons in the title bar. When you click on any of the buttons, the corresponding action is invoked.

8
Kendo UI Mobile Framework

In this chapter, we will cover the following recipes:

- ▶ Creating a layout and adding views to the layout
- ▶ Setting the initial layout and view when initializing the application
- ▶ Using the Application object to navigate to various views
- ▶ Adding touch events to your mobile application

Introduction

In the earlier recipes, we looked at various components available in the Kendo UI library that enable you to build web applications rapidly. In the upcoming recipes, we will take a look at the Kendo UI Mobile library that provides an application framework and a set of widgets that enable you to build mobile applications quickly. The Kendo UI Mobile framework renders the application by providing a native look and feel on various mobile platforms, which includes iOS, Android, Blackberry, and Windows Phone 8. The developers can focus on delivering functionality and depend on the Mobile framework to provide the native look and feel of various platforms, thereby reducing the development effort and maintaining the same code base for all the platforms.

Creating a layout and adding views to the layout

Every Kendo Mobile application has one or more layouts and multiple views added to it. Both the layout and view are widgets, that is, visual components that can be used to build a mobile application. There are several such widgets, which we will explore in the next chapter. In this recipe, we will take a look at building a simple application by creating a layout and adding multiple views to it.

Getting started

There are separate CSS and JS files that need to be included when working with mobile applications. The CSS file should refer to the `kendo.mobile.all.min.css` file located in the `styles` directory and the JS files should refer to `kendo.mobile.min.js`, located in the `js` directory.

Also, the reference to the jQuery library should remain as it is, that is, the Kendo UI Mobile library (`kendo.mobile.min.js`) has a dependency on jQuery.

How to do it...

As mentioned in the previous section, let's first include the CSS and JS files references in the HTML page, as shown in the following code snippet:

```
<link rel="stylesheet"
      type="text/css"
      href="../../styles/kendo.mobile.all.min.css">

<script src="../../js/jquery.min.js"></script>

<script src="../../js/kendo.mobile.min.js"></script>
```

 You might have to adjust the paths of the file based on the directory structure of your development environment.

The next step is to create a layout. A layout serves as a container for various views in the application. A layout defines the structure of the application; it contains widgets that will remain constant while the user is interacting with the application. For example, most of the applications have a header and a footer that remain constant while navigating through the application. The header and footer widgets can be a part of the layout and the dynamic part, that is, views that change based on the state of the application will be associated with a layout. Views can be considered as individual pages in the application that are displayed based on the state of the application. For example, you can have two views, namely, login and register. Based on the application state, one of these views is rendered. Create a layout widget using the `div` element by adding data attributes:

```
<div
   data-role="layout"
   data-id="defaultLayout">

</div>
```

Here, the `data-role` attribute is set to the layout, identifying the element as a layout widget. Every widget in the Mobile framework will have the `data-role` attribute set to the corresponding widget name. The `data-id` attribute is used to identify the widget on the page. There can be multiple layout widgets in the page, and each widget needs to have a unique ID that identifies the widget in the application.

Now let's add a couple of widgets to the layout, such as a `header` widget, which contains a `navbar`, and a `footer` widget, which contains `tabstrip`:

```
<div
   data-role="layout"
   data-id="defaultLayout">

<header data-role="header">

  <div data-role="navbar">
    Application Header
  </div>

</header>
```

```
    <footer data-role="footer">

      <div data-role="tabstrip">

        <a data-icon="about">About</a>

        <a data-icon="settings">Settings</a>

      </div>

    </footer>
  </div>
```

As mentioned earlier, a widget is created by assigning appropriate values to the `data-role` attribute. In this case, the `header`, `navbar`, `footer`, and `tabstrip` values are assigned to the `data-role` attribute of various elements.

Once a layout is added to the page, the next step would be to add a view. A `view` widget represents a single view that needs to be shown when the application is rendered. There can be multiple views in the page and only one view can be rendered at any given point, depending on the state of the application:

```
<div
  data-role="view"
  data-layout="defaultLayout">

  Hello Kendo!!
</div>
```

Here, apart from the `data-role` attribute, the `div` element also has a `data-layout` attribute. The `data-layout` attribute is used to associate the `view` widget with a `layout` widget in the page. In this case, the value of the `data-layout` attribute is `defaultLayout`, which is the value of the `data-id` attribute of the `layout` widget. The `header` and `footer` widgets defined in `layout` are positioned accordingly, and the `View` widget is rendered in the available space inside the layout. The last step would be to initialize the application. To initialize it, include the following code snippet:

```
<script>
  var app = new kendo.mobile.Application();
</script>
```

The preceding code snippet will initialize all the widgets in the page and make associations between the layout and views. The Application object can then be used to route between multiple views in the page, and we will visit this scenario in the upcoming recipes.

How it works...

When you execute the page, you will see a navigational bar and a tab strip in the header and footer of the page. Also, the **Hello Kendo!!** message will be shown in the body of the page.

The following screenshot shows you how the application will look when you view the page on an iPhone that runs iOS7:

Notice that there was no extra code written to set the look and feel of the application. The Mobile framework provides this functionality out of the box, that is, it determines the user agent and adds CSS classes to the elements in the page.

When you inspect the page, you will see classes added to the body tag, as shown in the following line of code:

```
<body class="km-on-ios km-ios7 km-7 km-m0 km-web km-black-status-
    bar km-vertical km-widget km-pane" data-role="pane" style="">
```

Notice the `km-on-ios` and `km-ios7` class added to the body tag. If you view the same page on an Android device, it would be rendered differently.

Again, the framework determines the user agent and adds CSS classes to the body tag. In this case, it would be as shown in the following code snippet:

```
<body class="km-on-android km-android km-4 km-m0 km-web km-black-
   status-bar km-vertical km-widget km-pane" data-role="pane"
   style="">
```

Here, the `km-on-android` and `km-android` classes are added.

There's more...

The Mobile framework renders the application based on the device it is accessed from. However, in scenarios where you want to customize the layout for a given platform, you can specify the `data-platform` attribute. For example, you can specify `data-platform` as the iOS for the previous layout and add another layout to the page with its `data-platform` attribute set to `android`:

```
<div
  data-role="layout"
  data-id="defaultLayout"
  data-platform="android">

  <footer data-role="footer">

    <div data-role="tabstrip">

      <a data-icon="about">About</a>

      <a data-icon="settings">Settings</a>

      <a data-icon="share">Share</a>

      <a data-icon="refresh">Refresh</a>

    </div>

  </footer>
</div>
```

 The `tabstrip` widget has two additional icons. When you access the application from an Android device, the previous layout would be selected by the framework.

Setting the initial layout and view when initializing the application

When working on complex mobile applications, you will have multiple layouts and views in the page. In this case, the initial view to render within a selected layout would not be possible to determine. However, options can be passed to the `kendo.mobile.application` function to set the layout and the initial view to use when the application is initialized.

How to do it...

Let's consider that there are two layouts and two views in the page. The layouts differ by the number of elements in `tabstrip`. In `layout1`, let's consider the header text, which reads `Layout1 header` and has two elements in its `tabstrip`:

```
<div
  data-role="layout"
```

```
      data-id="layout1">

      <!-- header here -->

      <footer data-role="footer">

        <div data-role="tabstrip">

          <a data-icon="about">About</a>

          <a data-icon="settings">Settings</a>

        </div>

      </footer>
    </div>
```

In the same page, there will be another layout with the `data-id` attribute set to `layout2`. This layout's header text would read `Layout2 header`, and the footer would contain four elements in its `tabstrip`:

```
<div
  data-role="layout"
  data-id="layout2">

      <!-- header here -->

      <footer data-role="footer">

        <div data-role="tabstrip">

          <a data-icon="about">About</a>

          <a data-icon="settings">Settings</a>

          <a data-icon="share">Share</a>

          <a data-icon="refresh">Refresh</a>

        </div>

      </footer>
    </div>
```

The next step is to add views to the page. Let's add two views and specify the id attribute for them:

```
<div
  data-role="view"
  id="view1">

  From View1

</div>

<div
  data-role="view"
  id="view2">

  From View2

</div>
```

Notice that the views in this page do not have the data-layout attribute. When the page is rendered, you would see that the first view in the page (with id='view1') is rendered without any layout. To change this behavior, you can specify the layout and the initial view to use when initializing the application:

```
<script>
  var app = new kendo.mobile.Application(document.body, {
    layout: 'layout2',
    initial: 'view2'
  });
</script>
```

Here, the first argument of the kendo.mobile.Application function is document.body. The first argument of this function is the target element. It is usually the container for various widgets (the element with the data-role attribute). The second argument is an object that contains a set of options used to initialize the application. Here, we will specify the layout and the initial view to use when rendering the page.

How it works...

When you render the page, you would see that `layout2` is used when rendering `view2`.

If you specify the `data-layout` attribute for the view element, then the view would be rendered with that layout instead of the one mentioned when initializing the application.

There's more...

In the previous recipe, it was mentioned that the `data-platform` attribute is used to specify the platform for which the layout is built. In many scenarios, you might like the same look and feel to appear in all the platforms. For example, if you are using an iOS device and would like to force the look and feel of Android, then you can specify the attribute platform when initializing the application:

```
<script>
  var app = new kendo.mobile.Application(document.body, {
    layout: 'layout2',
    initial: 'view2',
```

```
      platform: 'android'
   });
</script>
```

Now when you render the page on any device, you should be able to see the same look and feel across all platforms.

Using the Application object to navigate to various views

When building a mobile application, you will have multiple views representing various states in the application, that is, each state is represented by a `View` component in the application. For example, when you click on a button, the current view is disposed and the new view should be displayed. The Application object is used to navigate between various views in the application. These views can be defined in the same HTML document or can be present as a separate document (partials).

How to do it...

A good way to structure the code is to create multiple pages and separate the views. Specifying all the views in the same page will increase the size of the response and, hence, hamper the performance. Let's create a page that contains two buttons, namely, **Login** and **Register**:

```
<div
  data-role="layout"
  data-id="layout1">

  <header data-role="header">

    <div data-role="navbar">
      <span data-role="view-title"></span>
    </div>

  </header>
</div>

<div
  data-role="view"
  data-layout="layout1"
```

```
      data-title="Home">

    <a
      data-role="button"
      id="loginBtn"
      class="button">

      Login

    </a>
    <a
      data-role="button"
      id="registerBtn"
      class="button">

      Register

    </a>
  </div>
```

Let's call this page the **Home** page. It contains a `layout` widget and a `view` widget. The view contains two buttons. Notice that the layout's `navbar` widget contains a `span` element with the `data-role` attribute set to `view-title`. This allows various views to provide a title that will be displayed in the `navbar` widget. The `view` widget specifies the `data-title` attribute with its value as `Home`. This will set the layout's `navbar` text with the same value.

The view contains two buttons: **Login** and **Register**. The next step is to define views that will be displayed when you click on one of these buttons; the following code snippet shows you a description of `Login View`:

```
<div
  data-role="layout"
  data-id="login-layout">

  <header data-role="header">

    <div data-role="navbar">
      <a
        class="nav-button"
        data-role="backbutton"
        data-align="left">
        Back
```

```
    </a>

    <span data-role="view-title"></span>
  </div>

</header>

</div>


<div
  data-role="view"
  data-layout="login-layout"
  data-title="Login">

  Login Page

</div>
```

The preceding code snippet is placed in the `login.html` file. Here, the layout is similar to the one created in the **Home** page, except that it now contains a **Back** button (`data-role=backbutton`). The `backbutton` widget is used as a navigation widget to navigate back to the previous page. A similar page, `register.html`, is created and contains the same layout and view.

The next step is to bind the buttons in the **Home** page to these pages. The Application object is used to navigate between various pages. Let's add event handlers to the login and register buttons on the page:

```
<script>
  var app = new kendo.mobile.Application();

  $('#loginBtn').on('click', function () {
    app.navigate('login.html');
  });

  $('#registerBtn').on('click', function () {
    app.navigate('register.html');
  });

</script>
```

The `navigate` method is used to navigate to different pages. When the user clicks on any of these buttons, the `navigate` method on the Application object is called to navigate to the corresponding page.

How it works...

When you render the page (**Home** page), there are two buttons, **Login** and **Register**.

On clicking on the **Login** button, the user would be navigated to the `login.html` page, and when you click on the **Register** button, you would be navigated to the `register.html` page. The screenshot of the **Login** page is shown as follows:

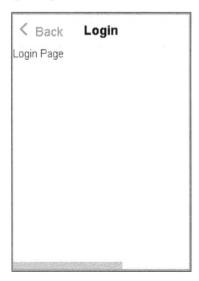

The `navbar` title is updated, and it has a **Back** button. On clicking on the **Back** button, the user is navigated to the **Home** page. On the **Home** page, when you click on the **Register** button, the registration page, that is, the `register.html` page, is shown as follows:

The **Register** view also contains the **Back** button, allowing the user to navigate to the **Home** page.

There's more...

When navigating from one view to the other, you can specify the transition effects that can be applied.

Specifying view transitions

When transitioning from one view to the other, you can specify the transition effect that needs to be applied using the `data-transition` attribute. The following values can be set as values of the `data-transition` attribute:

- ► `slide`: This transition effect slides the old view content to the left and inserts the new view content slides in its place. You can specify the direction using the slide (direction). By default, the direction is left; the other option is right.
- ► `zoom`: Here, the new view content zooms from the center of the old view. The old view content will fade out and the new view content will be shown.

- ▸ `fade`: Using this effect, the new content fades in on top of the old view. The old view content will fade out, showing you the content from the new view.

- ▸ `overlay`: The `overlay` effect is similar to the `slide` effect, except that the previous view remains under the new one. The transition direction can be specified using `overlay` (direction). By default, the direction is left; other supported directions include right, up, and down.

In all of the transition effects mentioned, the content along with its header and footer is shown. It is also possible to specify the transition effect for the entire application instead of specifying the `data-transition` attribute for each `view` widget in the document. When initializing the application using the Application object, specify the `transition` property with the desired effect as its value:

```
var app = new kendo.mobile.Application(document.body, {
  transition: "zoom"
});
```

This allows the `transition` effect to be applied to the entire application.

Adding touch events to your mobile application

The Kendo UI Mobile framework provides various APIs to handle touch-based events. The applications that you build should not only allow the user to perform regular select events on the touch interface, but they should also handle various touch gestures such as double tap, swipe, and drag-and-drop. In this recipe, we will take a look at the various touch events that can be added.

How to do it...

For the purpose of this example, let's consider the same layout used in the previous recipe and add a view to the page. The content of this view would be a `touch` widget that specifies an area in the view enabled for touch events:

```
<div
  data-role="view"
  data-layout="defaultLayout">
  <div
    id="touchSurface"
    data-role="touch"
    data-enable-swipe="1"
```

```
    data-touchstart="touchstart"
    data-swipe="swipe"
    data-tap="tap"
    data-doubletap="doubletap"
    data-hold="hold"
    style="height: 200px;">

    Touch Surface

  </div>
</div>
```

In addition to the `data-role` attribute being set to `touch`, the widget includes various data attributes that specify the touch event handlers. This includes `touchstart`, `swipe`, `tap`, `double tap`, and `hold`. The value assigned to these data attributes are names of the event handlers. These event handlers would be defined in the `script` tag. Notice that there is an attribute, `data-enable-swipe`, set to 1, indicating that the swipe feature is enabled:

```
<script>
  var app = new kendo.mobile.Application();


  function touchstart(event) {
    console.log('Event - Touch Start' + " X=
      "+event.touch.x.location + " Y= " + event.touch.y.location);
  }
  function tap(event) {
    console.log('Event - Tap');
  }
  function doubletap(event) {
    console.log('Event - Double tap');
  }
  function hold(event) {
    console.log('Event - Hold');
  }
  function swipe(event) {
    console.log('Swipe direction ' + event.direction);
  }
</script>
```

How it works...

The touchstart event is invoked when the user touches the surface. The event object available in the touchstart event handler can be used to determine the x and y coordinates where the touch was triggered. The tap event is invoked when the user taps on the screen, that is, after lifting the finger from the touch screen. Similarly, a doubletap event is invoked when the user taps on the screen twice in quick succession. If the user touches the screen and does not lift his finger for a few seconds, then the hold event is fired. The swipe event is fired when the users swipes his finger either from left to right or from right to left. The direction attribute available on the event object can be used to determine the direction in which the user has initiated the swipe. The sequence of events is as follows:

- ▶ The touchstart event will be triggered when the user touches the screen
- ▶ The tap event will be triggered when the user taps on the screen
- ▶ The doubletap event will be invoked after tap when the application recognizes the second tap

In the case of hold, the following sequence is executed:

- ▶ The touchstart event will be triggered
- ▶ The hold event will be triggered when the user continues his focus on one point for a long time

9

Kendo UI Mobile Widgets

In this chapter, we will cover the following recipes:

- ▶ Creating a list using a ListView widget
- ▶ Binding the ListView widget to a DataSource object
- ▶ Fixing the headers when the user scrolls through the list
- ▶ Filtering the elements in the ListView widget
- ▶ Building a hierarchical list using the ListView widget
- ▶ Building an endless scrolling list
- ▶ Showing a list of actions that can be performed using the ActionSheet widget
- ▶ Using the ScrollView widget to navigate through a collection of pictures
- ▶ Creating a SplitView widget to display multiple panes in a tablet and building interaction between the panes
- ▶ Using a TabStrip widget to display different views

Introduction

The Kendo UI Mobile library contains a multitude of widgets that can be readily used in your mobile applications. These widgets allow you to build some of the common mobile-related workflows by configuring them to match your needs. Some of the commonly used widgets include ListView, ScrollView, ActionSheet, TabStrip, and Navbar. The library also provides a SplitView widget that can be used in tablet applications.

In this chapter, we will see how to create ListView that displays a flat or hierarchical collection of data; then, visit some of the configuration options that can be used to achieve some of the workflows, for example, building an endless scrolling list. The ActionSheet widget is then used to perform an action on the selected list element. We will also see how a gallery-like application can be created using the ScrollView widget. The SplitView widget is used in tablets to display two different views in a single page and bind the interaction between them.

Creating a list using a ListView widget

The ListView widget allows you to display a list of items on the page. This list can be flat or grouped. The list values can be specified in the HTML markup, or the ListView widget can be bound to a `DataSource` object. In this recipe, we will take a look at creating a ListView widget where the list values are specified in the markup.

How to do it...

A ListView widget can be created using an unordered or ordered list. To create a ListView widget, assign the `listview` value to the `data-role` attribute:

```
<ul
  data-role="listview">

  <li>
    <a href="her.html">
      <img src="./images/her.jpg" />
      Her
    </a>
  </li>
  <li>
    <a href="gravity.html">
      <img src="./images/gravity.jpg" />

    </a>
  </li>
  <li>
    <a href="12_years_a_slave.html">
      <img src="./images/12_years_a_slave.jpg" />
      12 Years A Slave
```

```
        </a>
      </li>
      .
      .
      .
    </ul>
```

The preceding markup contains an unordered list, where each list element contains an image and a text. When the application is initialized, the widgets that are present in the page are initialized based on the values assigned to the `data-role` attribute.

How it works...

When you render the page, the ListView widget is constructed and rendered on the mobile device, as shown in the following screenshot:

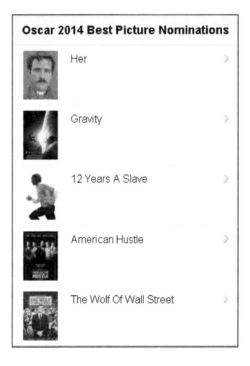

Here, each list item contains an `anchor` (hyperlink to a page) element whose `href` attribute refers to the `html` page. Also, it contains a right arrow aligned to the right-hand side of each item in the list. This indicates that the user can click to view the details for that particular item in the list.

When you click on the list element, you will be navigated to the corresponding page.

Her

A lonely writer develops an unlikely relationship with his newly purchased operating system that's designed to meet his every need.

Director: Spike Jonze
Cast: Joaquin Phoenix, Amy Adams, Scarlett Johansson

There's more...

A ListView widget integrates with a DetailsButton widget that can be used to add an icon to the right-hand side of each element in the list. This icon is added to mention the action that can be performed on the list item.

To add `detailbutton` for the list element, insert an `anchor` element with the `data-role` attribute set to `detailbutton`. Also, you need to specify the `data-style` attribute that specifies the type of detail button being added. Detail buttons support four styles: `contactadd`, `detaildisclose`, `rowinsert`, and `rowdelete`.

You can also add custom icons by specifying the `data-icon` attribute instead of `data-style`:

```
<ul
  data-role="listview">

  <li>
    Contact Add
```

```
        <a data-role="detailbutton"
          data-style="contactadd">
        </a>
    </li>
    <li>
      Detail Disclose
      <a data-role="detailbutton"
      data-style="detaildisclose">
      </a>
    </li>
    <li>
      Row Insert
      <a data-role="detailbutton"
        data-style="rowinsert">
      </a>
    </li>
    <li>
      Row Delete
      <a data-role="detailbutton"
        data-style="rowdelete">
      </a>
    </li>
    <li>
      Battery (Custom Icon)
      <a data-role="detailbutton"
        data-icon="battery">
      </a>
    </li>

  </ul>
```

Here, the last element in the ListView widget contains an anchor with the `data-icon` attribute set to `battery`. You can assign the following values to the `data-icon` attribute: about, action, add, bookmarks, camera, cart, compose, contacts, details, downloads, fastforward, favorites, featured, toprated, globe, history, home, info, more, mostrecent, mostviewed, organize, pause, play, recents, refresh, reply, rewind, search, settings, share, stop, and trash.

When you render the page, you will see detail buttons added to the right-hand side of each list element.

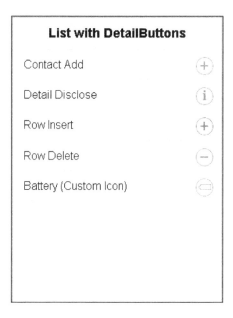

You can also add a custom icon by specifying the value of the data-icon attribute as custom and adding the km-custom class to the CSS style sheet.

Binding the ListView widget to a DataSource object

As mentioned in the previous recipe, a ListView widget can be created either by specifying the list elements in the markup or by binding it to a DataSource object. In this recipe, we will look at how ListView is populated using the DataSource object.

How to do it...

Let's create an empty list that will then be populated with data from a DataSource object:

```
<ul
    id="listViewContainer">

</ul>
```

Notice that the unordered list does not specify the data-role attribute. A ListView widget can be initialized by invoking the kendoMobileListView function on the DOM element:

```
var listElements = ['Her', 'Gravity', '12 Years A Slave',
                    'Captain Phillips', 'American Hustle',
                    'The Wolf Of Wall Street', 'Nebraska',
                    'Dallas Buyers Club', 'Philomena'];

$('#listViewContainer').kendoMobileListView({
  dataSource: listElements
});
```

The **listElements** array contains a set of strings that will then be used as a dataSource to populate the ListView widget. The kendoMobileListView function is used to initialize the list element. The dataSource option is specified when initializing the widget.

Alternatively, dataSource can also refer to a remote service that returns an array of strings:

```
$('#listViewContainer').kendoMobileListView({
  dataSource: {
    transport: {
      read: '/services/listViewService'
    }
  }
});
```

How it works...

When you render the page, the ListView widget is initialized and is populated with data that is present in the array. If DataSource refers to a service URL, a GET request is sent to the service and the data returned by the service is used to populate the ListView widget.

Oscar 2014 Best Picture Nominations

Her

Gravity

12 Years A Slave

Captain Phillips

American Hustle

The Wolf Of Wall Street

Nebraska

Dallas Buyers Club

Philomena

There's more...

In the preceding recipe, we have populated a ListView widget with values in an array. You can also provide a template that can be used when populating the list with a `DataSource` object.

Let's create an array of objects, where each object contains two properties, `name` and `image`, as follows:

```
var listElements = [
  {name: 'Her', image: 'her.jpg'},
  {name: 'Gravity', image: 'gravity.jpg'},
  {name: '12 Years A Slave', image: '12_years_a_slave.jpg'},
  {name: 'Captain Phillips', image: 'captain_phillips.jpg'},
  {name: 'American Hustle', image: 'american_hustle.jpg'},
  {name: 'The Wolf Of Wall Street',
image: 'wolf_of_wall_street.jpg'},
  {name: 'Nebraska', image: 'nebraska.jpg'},
  {name: 'Dallas Buyers Club',
   image: 'dallas_buyers_club.jpg'},
  {name: 'Philomena', image: 'philomena.jpg'}
];
```

The next step is to create a template that will be used when populating the list:

```
<script type="text/x-kendo-template" id="list-template">
  <a>
    <img src="./images/#= image #" />
    #= name #
  </a>
</script>
```

The template specifies a placeholder for the `image` and `name` properties. Now when you initialize the widget, in addition to specifying the `dataSource` property, specify the `template` property:

```
$('#listViewContainer').kendoMobileListView({
  dataSource: listElements,
  template: $('#list-template').html()
});
```

The `template` property here contains a reference to the template specified earlier (id=#list-template); this template is compiled against the data present in the `dataSource` object. For each object in the `dataSource` object, a list element is generated and appended to the ListView widget.

Fixing the headers when the user scrolls through the list

The items in the ListView widget can be grouped by a property. For example, assume that the list contains a set of names or contacts in your directory. These contacts can be grouped by the letter the contact name begins with. When you render the list, you would see that these contacts are grouped and on scrolling, the header is fixed.

How to do it...

To create fixed headers, that is, data grouped by a particular attribute, each object in the collection or the array should include that attribute. Let's create a sample array where each object contains two properties, `name` and `startsWith`; the `startsWith` attribute will be used to group the names in the list:

```
var actors = [
  {"name": "Leonardo DiCaprio", "startsWith": "L"},
  {"name": "Johnny Depp", "startsWith": "J"},
  {"name": "Al Pacino", "startsWith": "A"},
  {"name": "Bradley Cooper", "startsWith": "B"},
  {"name": "Tom Cruise", "startsWith": "T"},
  {"name": "Jude Law", "startsWith": "J"},
  {"name": "Robert Downey Jr.", "startsWith": "R"},
  {"name": "Will Smith", "startsWith": "W"},
  {"name": "Robert De Niro", "startsWith": "R"},
  {"name": "Antonio Banderas", "startsWith": "A"},
  {"name": "Christian Bale", "startsWith": "C"},
  {"name": "Brad Pitt", "startsWith": "B"},
  {"name": "Tom Hanks", "startsWith": "T"},
  {"name": "Robert Pattinson", "startsWith": "R"},
  {"name": "Ben Stiller", "startsWith": "B"}
];
```

Note that the list is not in a sorted order; we will use this list as a `DataSource` for a ListView widget:

```
function mobileListViewInit () {
  $('#listViewContainer').kendoMobileListView({
    dataSource: kendo.data.DataSource.create({
      data: actors,
```

```
        group: 'startsWith'
    }),

    template: '#= name #',
    fixedHeaders: true
  });
}
```

In the preceding code snippet, the `mobileListViewInit` function is used to initialize the ListView widget. This function is invoked when the `view` that contains the ListView widget is initialized. The `view` should specify the `data-init` attribute that refers to the `mobileListViewInit` function as its value. The `dataSource` property is used to provide the input data (that refers to the `actors` array), and it also specifies the `group` property whose value is `startsWith`. Apart from the `dataSource` property, the list's `view` initialization also contains the `template` and `fixedHeaders` properties. The `fixedHeaders` property is used to fix the header for each list group when the user scrolls the list.

How it works...

When the ListView widget is initialized, the names in the array are grouped by the `startsWith` property, and you will see the names in ascending order, that is, the names are listed in alphabetical order, as shown in the following screenshot:

Now when the user scrolls down, you will see that the corresponding headers stick to the top, indicating that the current list that is at the top of the list is that of a particular group.

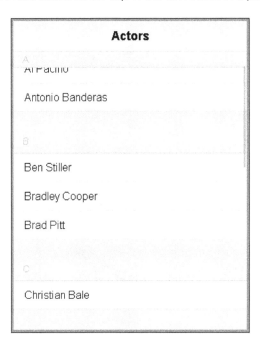

In the preceding screenshot, the user has scrolled down but the header is at the top of the page, indicating that the current list starts with the letter **A**. The `fixedHeaders` property will fix the header when the user scrolls down the list.

Filtering the elements in ListView

The ListView widget can contain several list elements, and scrolling through the entire list to get to the desired list element would be time consuming. For example, consider your contacts list; to get to a particular contact, one will have to scroll several times. To obliterate this, you can add a filter and use it to retrieve the desired list element that matches the input text.

How to do it...

Let's consider a flat data source, that is, an array that contains a list of strings:

```
var listElements = ['Leonardo DiCaprio', 'Johnny Depp',
                    'Bradley Cooper', 'Al Pacino',
                    'Tom Cruise','Jude Law',
```

```
                           'Robert Downey Jr.', 'Will Smith',
                           'Robert De Niro', 'Christian Bale',
                           'Brad Pitt','Tom Hanks',
                           'Robert Pattinson', 'Ben Stiller'];
```

Now when initializing the ListView widget, provide the preceding elements as a `dataSource` and also include a `filterable` attribute and set its value to `true`:

```
$('#listViewContainer').kendoMobileListView({
   dataSource: listElements,
   filterable: true
});
```

When you set the `filterable` attribute to `true`, a search input field is added to the top of the list. When the user starts to type in the search input field, the list is filtered to show the options that match the user input. Here, the user input string is compared with elements in the list and only those that start with the input string are displayed in the list. If you would like to change this logic so that it returns those elements that contain the input string instead of the ones that start with it, then mention the `operator` field as follows:

```
$('#listViewContainer').kendoMobileListView({
   dataSource: listElements,
   filterable: {
      "operator": "contains"
   }
});
```

The `operator` field can contain one of these values: `startsWith`, `endswith`, `contains`, `eq` (equal to), `neq` (not equal to), `lt` (less than), `lte` (less than or equal to), `gt` (greater than), and `gte` (greater than or equal to).

When working with `dataSource`, which contains objects, the widget would fail to filter the list because it wouldn't know the field against which the user input has to be matched. To fix this, you can specify the `field` option:

```
$('#listViewContainer').kendoMobileListView({
   dataSource: actors,
   template: '#= name #',
   filterable: {
      "field": "name",
      "operator": "contains"
   }
});
```

The preceding code snippet looks for the—name field and filters out the elements in the list. In all the previous cases, the list is filtered out as and when the user starts to type in the search input field. If you would like the user to click on the search button, then specify the autoFilter option and set it to false:

```
$('#listViewContainer').kendoMobileListView({
  dataSource: actors,
  template: '#= name #',
  filterable: {
    "field": "name",
    "autoFilter": false,
    "operator": "contains"
  }
});
```

By setting the autoFilter property to false, the user will have to hit the search button to get the filtered list. This is useful when you are working with a long list and don't want the list to refresh on every key input.

How it works...

When you render the page, you will see the search input field at the top of the list.

When you start to key in the search field, the list is filtered, and it contains only those options that start with the input text.

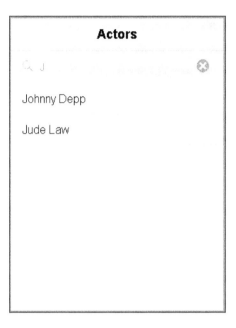

When you change the operator to `contains`, the list is filtered out and it now has those options that contain the input text.

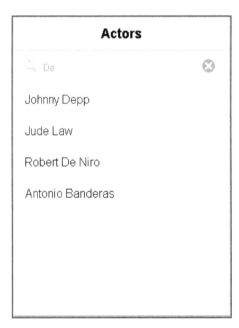

There's more...

The search input field has a placeholder text, **Search**. You can customize this text by specifying the `placeholder` option:

```
$('#listViewContainer').kendoMobileListView({
  dataSource: actors,
  template: '#= name #',
  filterable: {
    "field": "name",
    "autoFilter": false,
    "placeholder": "Find...",
    "operator": "contains"
  }
});
```

When you render the page, you will see that the `placeholder` text has changed to **Find...**.

Building a hierarchical list using the ListView widget

In all the previous recipes, the data returned from the service contained all the records, and the same were displayed in the list. When working with a hierarchical data structure instead of a flat one, the ListView widget can be customized so that it can display the data in a hierarchical way, that is, displaying the elements in the first level of the hierarchy and then traversing through various levels until the leaf nodes in the hierarchy are reached.

Getting started

To build a hierarchical list, the service should return data that lists the first set of records that need to be displayed. Each record should have a field that indicates whether there are child records or it's a leaf node in the hierarchy. This information will then be used in the ListView widget, which would enable the user to navigate through the hierarchy.

How to do it...

The ListView widget should first display the records present in the top level of the hierarchy. Let's assume that the service is configured to return the same when it's queried from the client browser:

```
[
    {"id": 1, "name": "Lamborghini", "hasModels": true},
    {"id": 2, "name": "Ferrari", "hasModels": true},
    {"id": 3, "name": "Aston Martin", "hasModels": true}
]
```

The `id` property is used to uniquely identify each record in the hierarchical structure. It also has a `hasModels` property that indicates whether the record has child nodes associated with it. The next step is to create a `DataSource` object and specify the service URL as well as the schema details:

```
var cars  = new kendo.data.HierarchicalDataSource({
  transport: {
      read: '/carService'
  },

  schema: {
    model: {
      id: 'id',
      hasChildren: 'hasModels'
    }
  }
});
```

In the preceding code snippet, we are using `kendo.data.HierrachicalDataSource` to create an instance of hierarchical data source. The definition contains the schema object that specifies the mapping for the `id` and `hasChildren` properties. The `view` that renders the hierarchical structure should be used every time the user navigates to various levels in the hierarchy:

```
<div
  id="hierarchicalView"
  data-role="view"
  data-title="Cars"
  data-show="attachDataSource"
  data-layout="defaultLayout">

  <ul
    id="listViewContainer"
    data-role="listview"
    data-template="hierachicalTemplate">

  </ul>
</div>
```

The preceding `view` (with `id=hierarchicalView`) contains a ListView widget. The `view` specifies `data attribute - show`, whose value refers to the function that will be invoked every time `view` is rendered, that is, whenever `view` is reused to display the next level elements. The ListView widget specifies the `data-template` attribute as `hierarchicalTemplate`. The template can be specified when initializing the widget, or it can be specified as a `data-` attribute:

```
<script id="hierachicalTemplate" type="text/x-kendo-template">
  # if(data.hasModels) { #
    <a href="\#hierarchicalView?parent=#: data.id #">
      #= name #
    </a>
  # } else { #
    #= name #
  # } #
</script>
```

The template first checks whether the current model object (referred in data) has the `hasModels` property set to `true` and then adds a hyperlink that refers to the same `view` (with `id=hierarchicalView`) with a query parameter, `parent`, set to `id` of the model object. If the current model object is the leaf node, then the same would be added to the list without any hyperlink.

When the user clicks on the hyperlink, the view should be reused to display the next elements in the hierarchy. As mentioned earlier, the `data-show` attribute specifies the function that should be invoked every time the view is used to display the content. The `attachDataSource` function is invoked every time the view is shown:

```
function attachDataSource(e) {
    var parentID = e.view.params.parent,
    listView = $("#listViewContainer")
                            .data('kendoMobileListView');

    if (!parentID) {
        listView.setDataSource(cars);
    } else {
        cars.fetch(function () {
            var item = cars.get(parentID);
            listView.setDataSource(item.children);
        });
    }
}
```

Whenever the user clicks on the link, the view is reused and the preceding function is invoked. The event object is then used to get `parentID`. Initially, when the view is used to render the elements, that is, the elements in the top level in the hierarchy, `parentID` would be `null`. In this case, the ListView is set to the hierarchical data source that we defined earlier. When the user navigates the view, `parentID` would be present and the ListView's `dataSource` is set to the child nodes of the corresponding parent.

How it works...

When you render the page, the elements in the top level of the hierarchy would be displayed as shown in the following screenshot:

Here, since the `hasModels` property is set to true, all elements in the list are displayed along with a right arrow (**>**). This indicates that the user can navigate to the next set of nodes by clicking on it.

When the user clicks on any of the elements in ListView, the `attachDataSource` function is invoked. The clicked element's `id` would be used to get the next set of elements in the hierarchy. Note that the query parameter `parentID` is present when you have set the DataSource for the ListView; a GET request is sent to the service specifying the `parentID` value to the query parameter `id`. The remote service looks for the records and returns it. The request URL is of the form:

```
/service?id=<parentID>
```

When you click on the first element (`id = 1`), the service will look for the records whose `parentID` is 1. Let's assume that the service returns the following records:

```
[
    {"id": 11, "name": "Gallardo", "hasModels": false},
    {"id": 12, "name": "Aventador", "hasModels": false},
    {"id": 13, "name": "Huracan", "hasModels": false}
]
```

Notice that the value of `hasModels` is false in all the three objects. Now, view is updated to show the preceding records in ListView, and it does not contain the right arrow.

The template used to render the list elements checks the value of the `hasModels` property and adds an anchor element only if it's set to `true`. In this case, it's `false`, and hence it does not display the right arrow.

Building an endless scrolling list

A ListView widget can be customized to display an exhaustive list of items. There are multiple ways in which this can be done, for example, by adding a button at the bottom of the list, after clicking on which, the next set of elements would be added to the list. The other way would be to add more elements as and when the user scrolls down. This is called *endless scrolling* and it provides a seamless experience when the user is scrolling through an exhaustive list. In this recipe, we will see both the approaches, that is, adding a button to load more elements and creating an endless scrolling list, which is loaded when the user scrolls down.

How to do it...

In both the cases, the `DataSource` object must be configured so that it returns a limited number of records. While configuring `DataSource` for the ListView widget, specify the `pageSize` attribute:

```
dataSource: {
  transport: {
    read: '/movies/listService'
  },
  pageSize: 10
}
```

To add the button at the bottom of the list, specify the `loadMore` option with its value set to `true`:

```
function initListView (e) {
  $('#listViewContainer').kendoMobileListView({
    dataSource: {
      transport: {
        read: '/movies/listService'
      },
      pageSize: 10
    },

    loadMore: true

  });
}
```

To enable endless scrolling instead of adding the load more button, set the `endlessScroll` attribute to `true`:

```
function initListView (e) {
  $('#listViewContainer').kendoMobileListView({
    dataSource: {
      transport: {
        read: '/movies/listService'
      },
      pageSize: 10
    },

    endlessScroll: true

  });
}
```

How it works...

When you render the page, the button with the **Press to load more** text is shown at the bottom of the list, as shown in the following screenshot:

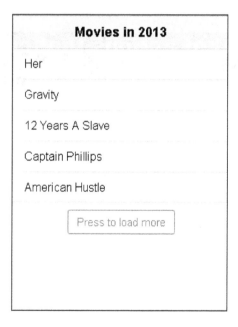

In case of an endless scrolling list, a request is sent to the service when the user scrolls down. While the list is being loaded, you will see the loader being shown, as depicted in the following screenshot:

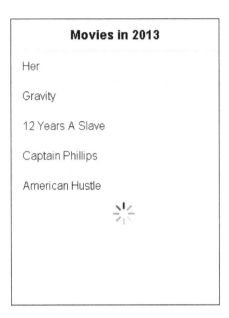

Showing a list of actions that can be performed using the ActionSheet widget

The Kendo Mobile ActionSheet widget is used to show you a list of actions that can be performed when a user taps on an element on the screen. The ActionSheet widget slides from the bottom and shows you a list of actions that can be performed against the tapped element on the screen.

How to do it...

Let's create `view`, which contains the ListView widget and an ActionSheet widget:

```
<div
  data-role="view"
  data-title="Movies to watch"
  data-layout="defaultLayout">

  <ul
```

```
        id="listViewContainer">



    </ul>

    <ul
      data-role="actionsheet"
      id="optionActionSheet">

      <li>
        <a data-action="option1">Favourite</a>
      </li>
      <li>
        <a data-action="option2">Watch</a>
      </li>
      <li>
        <a data-action="option3">Remove</a>
      </li>
    </ul>
  </div>
```

The content of the ListView widget is populated using a `DataSource` object. The ActionSheet widget (`ul` with `data-role=actionsheet`) contains a list of actions that need to be shown when the user clicks on any of the elements in the ListView widget. Notice that each list element contains an `anchor` element with a `data-action` attribute. This attribute is used to specify the JavaScript function to be invoked when the user clicks on the action button.

The next step is to associate elements in the list with the ActionSheet widget. To populate the elements in the list, `template` can be used and the same can specify the reference to the ActionSheet widget:

```
<script id="listViewTemplate" type="text/x-kendo-template">
  <a
    data-rel="actionsheet"
    href="\#optionActionSheet">

    #= data #

  </a>
</script>
```

Here, the anchor's `data-rel` attribute is set to `actionsheet`, and the `href` attribute refers to the ActionSheet widget (`id=optionActionSheet`).

How it works...

Each element in the ListView widget has a right arrow (**>**), which indicates that an action can be invoked on the list element:

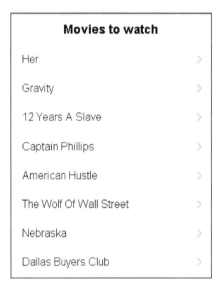

When you tap on any of the list elements, the ActionSheet widget is shown. The widget slides from the bottom of the screen and lists the options or actions that the user can perform, as shown in the following screenshot:

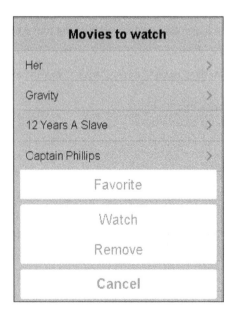

The overlay of the ActionSheet widget covers the entire screen and the list containing actions is shown. Notice that the ActionSheet widget, apart from listing the mentioned options, also includes the **Cancel** button.

When the user clicks on any of the previous options, the associated JavaScript function is invoked. On clicking on **Cancel**, the ActionSheet widget is hidden and the overlay is removed.

There's more...

The ActionSheet widget is shown as **Modal window** on an Android device. As mentioned earlier, the mobile widgets are customized to provide a native look and feel of various devices.

The options are listed with the **Cancel** option here as well.

Using the ScrollView widget to navigate through a collection of pictures

A ScrollView widget is used in picture galleries or carousel-like applications, where you would like to scroll to the next page to see the next picture in the gallery. The widget allows you to move to the next page or the previous page by swiping from right to left or left to right.

How to do it...

Let's create a `view` that contains a ScrollView widget:

```
<div
  data-role="view"
```

```
      data-title="Gallery"
      data-layout="defaultLayout">

      <div
        data-role="scrollview">

      </div>
    </div>
```

Here, a ScrollView widget is created inside the `view` by setting the `data-role` attribute to `scrollview`. The ScrollView widget now needs to contain pages that can be scrolled through by swiping from right to left or left to right. To create a page, add `div` elements inside the ScrollView container, and set the `data-role` attribute to `page`. Each page widget can then contain an image that needs to be shown:

```
<div
  data-role="scrollview">

  <div
    data-role="page">
      <img src="./images/large/her.jpg" />
  </div><div
    data-role="page">
    <img src="./images/large/gravity.jpg" />
  </div><div
    data-role="page">
    <img src="./images/large/12_years_a_slave.jpg" />
  </div><div
    data-role="page">
    <img src="./images/large/american_hustle.jpg" />
  </div><div
    data-role="page">
    <img src="./images/large/wolf_of_wall_street.jpg" />
  </div>
  .
  .
  .
</div>
```

How it works...

When you render the page, the ScrollView widget shows you the first page that contains the image.

Here, the ScrollView widget also includes `pager` at the bottom of the screen, which highlights the page that the user is on. When you swipe from right to left, the next page is shown as follows:

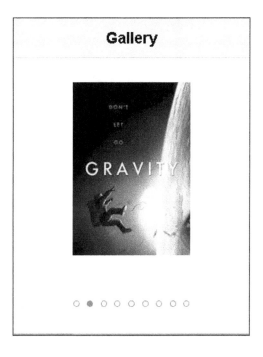

There's more...

When you render the page, the ScrollView widget shows you the first page in the set of pages by default. If you want to display a different page, then set the `data-page` attribute for the ScrollView widget element:

```
<div
    data-role="scrollview"
    data-page="4">

</div>
```

The page numbers are zero indexed, that is, when you specify the `data-page` attribute as 4, the fifth page in the list is shown.

If you want to hide the pager that is shown at the bottom of the ScrollView widget, then you can set the `data-enable-pager` attribute as `false`:

In the preceding screenshot, `pager` is removed; however, the user can still browse through the set of pages by swiping through it. This option is useful when you have an exhaustive list of pages to browse through, and showing a pager at the bottom of the screen would not be the experience that you want to provide.

Creating a SplitView widget to display multiple panes in a tablet and building interaction between the panes

The Kendo UI library provides a SplitView widget, which is a `tablet` specific widget. A SplitView widget consists of two or more `panes`, and each of these panes consist of one or more view widgets. Generally, the SplitView widget is used to select an item in the list in one pane and update the other pane that displays more data about the selected item.

How to do it...

Let's create two panes, **Left Pane** and **Right Pane**, and then include these `panes` inside a SplitView widget. Here's the markup for the **Left Pane**:

```
<div
   data-role="pane"
   id="nav-pane"
   data-layout="left-navbar-layout">

  <div
    data-role="view"
    id="test">

   <ul
      id="moviesList"
      data-role="listview"
      data-template="navbar-template">
   </ul>
  </div>

  <script type="text/x-kendo-template" id="navbar-template">
    <a href="\#movieDescription?movieID=#= data.id #"
      data-target="content-pane">
      #= data.name #
    </a>
  </script>

  <div
    data-role="layout"
```

```
        data-id="left-navbar-layout">

        <header data-role="header">

          <div data-role="navbar">
            Left Pane
          </div>

        </header>
      </div>

  </div>
```

A pane widget is created by setting the `data-role` attribute to `pane`. The pane contains a view widget and the view lists items that use a ListView widget. The view is associated with `Layout`, and the ListView widget is populated using the following `DataSource` object:

```
var listElements = [
  {id: 1, name: 'Her', image: 'her.jpg'},
  {id: 2, name: 'Gravity', image: 'gravity.jpg'},
  {id: 3, name: '12 Years A Slave', image:
    '12_years_a_slave.jpg'},
  {id: 4, name: 'Captain Phillips', image:
    'captain_phillips.jpg'},
  {id: 5, name: 'American Hustle', image: 'american_hustle.jpg'},
  {id: 6, name: 'The Wolf Of Wall Street', image:
    'wolf_of_wall_street.jpg'},
  {id: 7, name: 'Nebraska', image: 'nebraska.jpg'},
  {id: 8, name: 'Dallas Buyers Club', image: 'dallas_buyers_club.
jpg'},
  {id: 9, name: 'Philomena', image: 'philomena.jpg'}
];
```

Let's now consider the **Right Pane** widget that will be used to display details about the selected item in **Left Pane**:

```
<div
  data-role="pane"
  id="content-pane"
  data-layout="right-content-layout">

  <div
    data-role="view"
    data-show="displayOrders"
```

```
      id="movieDescription">


    <div id="movieDetails">

    </div>

  </div>

  <div
    data-role="layout"
    data-id="right-content-layout">

    <header data-role="header">
      <div data-role="navbar">
        Right Pane
      </div>
    </header>
  </div>

</div>
```

The **Right Pane** widget also contains the view; the content of this view is generated when the user selects an item in **Left Pane**. Notice that the anchor element specified in the Left pane template specifies the href attribute as \#movieDescription?movieID=#= data.id #, which refers to the view in **Right Pane**. Also, it specifies the data-target attribute as content-pane, which refers to **Right Pane** itself.

The next step would be to enclose the two panes inside a SplitView widget:

```
<div
  data-role="splitview">

  <div
    data-role="pane"
    id="nav-pane"
    data-layout="left-navbar-layout">
  .
  .
  .
  </div>
  <div
    data-role="pane"
```

```
        id="content-pane"
        data-layout="right-content-layout">
    .


    .
    </div>
</div>
```

The view widget in **Right pane** has the `data-show` attribute set to `displayOrders`; the `data-show` attribute is used to specify the JavaScript function that should be invoked when the view is used to show content. When the user clicks on any of the items in **Left Pane**, the view in **Right Pane** is used to display the details. Let's use the **Right Pane** widget to display the image of the selected element in **Left Pane**. The `displayOrder` function is implemented as follows:

```
function displayOrders (e) {
    var movieID = parseInt(e.view.params.movieID, 10);

    for (var i=0; i< listElements.length; i++) {
        if(listElements[i].id === movieID) {
            $('#movieDetails').html('<img src="images/large/' +
                listElements[i].image + '"/>');
            break;
        }
    }
}
```

Here, the function first gets d of the selected element and then gets the image of the corresponding element. This image is then shown in the view contained in **Right Pane**.

Similarly, whenever a user selects an item in the ListView present in **Left Pane**, the corresponding image would be shown in **Right Pane**.

How it works...

When you first render the page, the **Left Pane** widget is populated with the elements from `DataSource`.

Left Pane	Right Pane
Her 〉	
Gravity 〉	
12 Years A Slave 〉	
Captain Phillips 〉	
American Hustle 〉	
The Wolf Of Wall Street 〉	
Nebraska 〉	
Dallas Buyers Club 〉	
Philomena 〉	

Initially, **Right Pane** does not display any content since none of the items are selected in **Left Pane**. When you select any of the items from the ListView widget in **Left Pane**, the **Right Pane** widget is updated to show you the image:

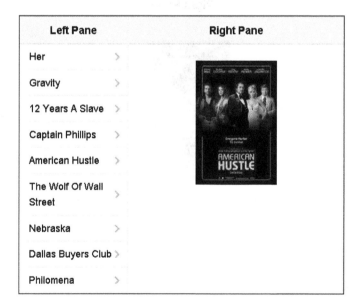

There's more...

The SplitView widget has stacked the panes horizontally; it's also possible to stack these panes vertically by specifying the `data-style` attribute to `vertical`:

```
<div
  data-role="splitview"
  data-style="vertical">
    .
    .
    .
</div>
```

The following screenshot is how the panes would look when they are stacked vertically:

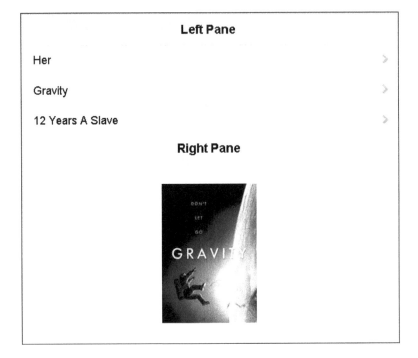

Tab between views in the application using a TabStrip widget

The TabStrip widget is used to navigate between various views in the application. TabStrip is usually placed in the footer of the layout, and on clicking the buttons present in TabStrip, the corresponding view is shown.

How to do it...

Let's create a layout that contains a TabStrip widget in the footer:

```
<div
  data-role="layout"
  data-id="defaultLayout">

  <footer data-role="footer">

    <div data-role="tabstrip">

      <a href="#contactsView"
      data-icon="about">
        Contacts
      </a>

      <a
        href="#favoritesView"
        data-icon="favorites">
        Favorites
      </a>

      <a
        href="#settingsView"
        data-icon="settings">
        Settings
      </a>

    </div>

  </footer>
</div>
```

In the preceding code snippet, the TabStrip widget (`data-role='tabstrip'`) contains three buttons: **Contacts**, **Favorites**, and **Settings**. Each of these buttons specify the `href` attribute whose value is the same as the value assigned to the `id` attribute of the `view` defined in the page.

The next step would be to define views that would get displayed when you select any of the buttons in `TabStrip`:

```html
<div
  id="contactsView"
  data-role="view"
  data-layout="defaultLayout">

  <ul
    id="contactsViewContainer"
    data-role="listview">
  </ul>
</div>

<div
  id="favoritesView"
  data-role="view"
  data-layout="defaultLayout">

  <ul
    id="favoritesViewContainer"
    data-role="listview">
  </ul>
</div>

<div
  id="settingsView"
  data-role="view"
  data-layout="defaultLayout">

  <ul
    data-role="listview">
    <li>Sorted
      <input type="check" data-role="switch" checked>
    </li>
    <li>Show Images
      <input type="check" data-role="switch">
    </li>
  </ul>
</div>
```

Notice that the `id` attribute of the preceding view widget definitions are referred in the `href` attribute of the `anchor` elements in the TabStrip widget.

How it works...

When you render the page, the **Contacts** view is shown, and the same is highlighted in the TabStrip widget:

Notice that the **Contacts** icon in TabStrip is highlighted, indicating that the current view shows you a list of **Contacts**. When you touch on the **Favorites** or **Settings** icon, the corresponding icon in TabStrip is highlighted and the view is also updated:

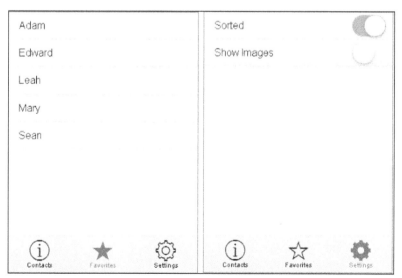

10
Kendo UI DataViz

In this chapter, we will cover the following recipes:

- ▸ Creating charts using `kendoChart`
- ▸ Binding a chart to a `DataSource` object
- ▸ Creating a multiaxis chart
- ▸ Displaying data over a period of time and using aggregate functions
- ▸ Making a chart interactive by adding events
- ▸ Changing the chart type dynamically

Introduction

The Kendo UI library provides a set of powerful visualization components that can be used to bring data to life. It uses modern browser technologies such as SVG and Canvas to render these charts. It falls back to VML on older browsers. The browser support ranges from IE7+ to Chrome, Firefox, Opera (15+), and Safari. In this chapter, we will look at building some of the basic charts such as the area chart, pie chart, and column chart, and how they can be customized. In the next chapter, we will look at some of the advanced data visualization charts that are used to build dashboard-like applications.

Creating charts using kendoChart

The Kendo data visualization library provides several charting widgets that can be built with ease. In this recipe, we will first build a column chart and then customize its look and feel. A column chart displays vertical bars, visually representing the provided data.

Getting started

The `kendo.all.min.js` file contains all the components, that is, Web, Mobile, and DataViz widgets. However, if you're building only data visualization components, then include the `kendo.dataviz.min.js` file.

How to do it...

To create a chart, let's add a container to the page, specifying the dimension of the chart area, as shown in the following line of code:

```
<div id="chart" style="width:500px; height: 400px">
```

Notice that the chart has a width of 500 pixels and a height of 400 pixels. This area will be used to render the chart. The next step is to initialize the chart using the `kendoChart` function, as shown in the following line of code:

```
$("#chart").kendoChart()
```

In the preceding code line, a chart is initialized by invoking the `kendoChart` function on the selected `div` element. When you render the page, a chart with only its axes will be shown. The next step is to provide some data and a set of options that will be used to display the chart. These includes the chart title and the type of chart that you want to display, as shown in the following code snippet:

```
$("#chart").kendoChart({
    title: {
        text: 'Browser Adoption'
    },
    categoryAxis: {
        categories: [2010, 2011, 2012, 2013, 2014]
    },
    series: [{
        name: 'Internet Explorer',
        data: ['32', '23', '17', '12', '9'],
        type: 'column'
    }],
    valueAxis: {
        labels: {
```

```
          format: '{0}%'
      }
   }
});
```

In the preceding code snippet, several options have been provided to initialize the chart widget. Let's take a look at each one of them:

- ▶ `title`: This option is used to specify the title text that should be shown on top of the chart. The text option specified in the title will be displayed.
- ▶ `categoryAxis`: This option is used to specify the categories that should be displayed on the *x* axis of the chart.
- ▶ `series`: This option is used to specify the data that needs to be displayed in the chart. The `name` option is used to display the legend information. The `data` option includes all the data that needs to be plotted on the chart and `type` specifies the chart type that needs to be displayed.
- ▶ `valueAxis`: This option refers to the *y* axis and in the preceding example, it specifies the format in which the values in the *y* axis should be displayed. The `{0}%` value serves as a template where `{0}` is replaced with a value based on the data that is provided.

How it works...

After providing all the options in the `kendoChart` function, you will see that a column chart is added to the page, which also contains the title and legend information, as shown in the following screenshot:

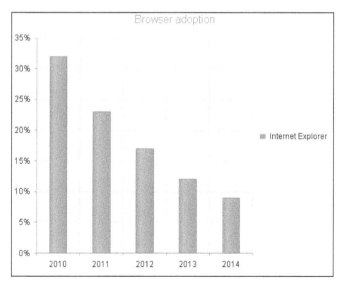

Notice that the preceding column chart shows you the title at the top and the legend information on the right-hand side. The color theme that has been applied is the default one.

There's more...

Charts can be used to show you series of data for multiple categories, and there are several options available to the user to customize the chart. Let's take a look at each one of these options in detail.

Showing multiple categories in the chart

The chart that we created had only one series added; when you want to compare multiple products or categories, the `series` array can include them:

```
series: [{
    name: 'Internet Explorer',
    data: ['32', '23', '17', '12', '9']
}, {
    name: 'Firefox',
    data: ['45', '39', '34', '28', '26']
}, {
    name: 'Chrome',
    data: ['15', '26', '40', '52', '56']
}, {
    name: 'Safari',
    data: ['6', '5', '4', '4', '4']
}]
```

Notice that the `type` information is removed from the series. When building a chart, you can specify the common options for the series under `seriesDefault`:

```
seriesDefaults: {
  type: 'column'
}
```

Now when you render the page, other series will be included.

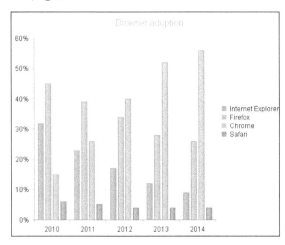

Changing the position of the title and legend information

It is possible to customize the chart to change the position of the title and legend information:

```
title: {
        text: 'Browser adoption',
        position: 'bottom'
    },
    legend: {
        position: 'bottom'
    }
```

When you render the page, the chart will occupy the entire width and the legend and title information will be shown below the chart.

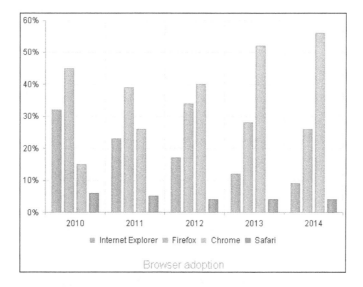

The height of the chart is affected and is now shown in the given height of 400 pixels in the chart along with the legend and title information. You can specify the position as top, bottom, right, left, or custom. When the position is custom, you need to specify the `offsetX` and `offsetY` options as well:

```
legend: {
    position: 'custom',
    offsetX: 50,
    offsetY: 20
}
```

Now when you render the page, you will notice that the legend information is positioned at 50 pixels from the left and 20 pixels from the top of the chart area, as shown in the following screenshot:

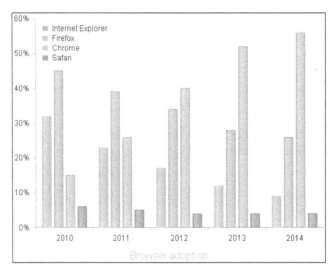

Changing the default theme

The theme applied in the preceding chart is the default one. You can change the theme from the default one by specifying the theme option, as shown in the following line of code:

```
theme: 'black'
```

After changing the theme to black, the page would be rendered as shown in the following screenshot:

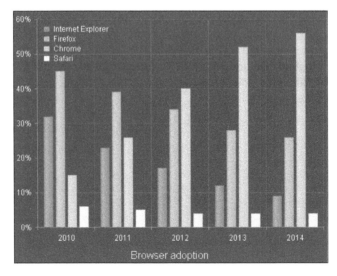

The other values that can be assigned to the `theme` property include `blueopal`, `bootstrap`, `highcontrast`, `metro`, `metroblack`, `moonlight`, `silver`, and `uniform`.

Binding a chart to a DataSource object

A Kendo chart widget can be bound to a `DataSource` object. This `DataSource` object can be `local` or `remoteDataSource`. When using a `DataSource` object, the `series` and `configurationAxis` fields must be configured to refer to the fields in the `DataSource` object.

How to do it...

Let's first create a local `DataSource` object, which will then be used to construct the chart:

```
var chromeBrowser = [{
    'year': 2008,
    'percentage': 0
}, {
    'year': 2009,
    'percentage': 4
}, {
    'year': 2010,
    'percentage': 15
}, {
    'year': 2011,
    'percentage': 26
}, {
    'year': 2012,
    'percentage': 40
}, {
    'year': 2013,
    'percentage': 52
}, {
    'year': 2014,
    'percentage': 56
}];
```

The next step is to specify the preceding code as a `DataSource` reference when constructing the chart:

```
$("#chart").kendoChart({
    dataSource: {
        data: chromeBrowser
    },
    title: {
```

```
        text: 'Chrome Browser adoption',
        position: 'bottom'
    },
    theme: 'blueOpal',
    seriesDefaults: {
        type: 'area'
    },
    categoryAxis: {
        field: 'year',
    },
    series: [{
        field: 'percentage'
    }],
    valueAxis: {
        labels: {
            format: '{0}%'
        }
    }
});
```

Here, `dataSource` in the preceding code snippet specifies a reference to the array of objects (`chromeBrowser`) that we defined earlier. The `categoryAxis` option specifies the `year` field, and the `series` field specifies the `percentage` field. The x axis now plots the year information and the y axis is projected with the percentage value in the `DataSource` object.

How it works...

In this example chart, the type of chart is specified as area, and now when you render the page, an area chart that shows the percentage adoption over several years is displayed, as shown in the following screenshot:

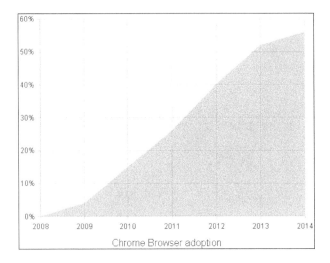

There's more...

In the preceding example, only one series was shown in the chart. When working with multiple series, the remote service needs to be configured to return data in a specific format.

Showing multiple series using the DataSource object

When you have multiple series to be added to the chart, the `DataSource` object should contain data grouped by category. In this example, the data is grouped by year, as shown in the following code snippet:

```
var browserAdoption = [{
    'year': 2011,
    'chrome': 40,
    'firefox': 30,
    'ie': 15,
    'safari': 15
}, {
    'year': 2012,
    'chrome': 45,
    'firefox': 25,
    'ie': 12,
    'safari': 18
}, {
    'year': 2013,
    'chrome': 50,
    'firefox': 22,
    'ie': 8,
    'safari': 20
}];
```

In our example, the `categoryAxis` option specifies the field as `year`; this will group the data by this field. The next step is to specify the previously mentioned configuration in the `series` option when constructing the chart:

```
series: [{
    field: 'chrome',
    name: 'Chrome'
}, {
    field: 'firefox',
    name: 'Firefox'
}, {
    field: 'safari',
    name: 'Safari'
```

```
}, {
    field: 'ie',
    name: 'IE'
}],
```

Now when you render the page, the series for various browsers is plotted on the chart, as shown in the following screenshot:

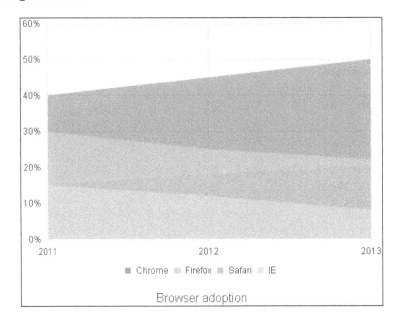

Showing values on the chart as labels

The chart can be customized to show you the values on the chart at specific points. The `labels` option is used to show you the value on the plotted chart:

```
seriesDefaults: {
    type: 'area',
    labels: {
        visible: true,
        format: '{0}%'
    }
}
```

Here, the `labels` option specifies two fields, namely, `visible` and `format`. The `labels` option for the series will add labels at the intersection of the *x* and *y* axes where the value is projected, as shown in the following screenshot:

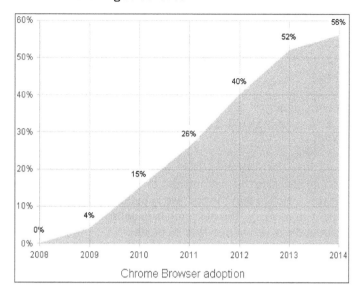

The preceding screenshot shows you the exact value of labels at the intersection of both the axes.

Creating a multiaxis chart

In many scenarios, you would like to group data by more than one field. In the examples depicted in the earlier recipes, the browser adoption data was grouped by year. Now, this data can be grouped by platform as well. For example, adoption of the Chrome browser in the year 2012 on the Windows platform can be accomplished by adding multiple axes to the chart.

How to do it...

The first step is to define the `series` data, which contains information grouped by platforms:

```
series: [{
    name: 'On Windows',
    data: ['15', '26', '40', '52', '56'],
    type: 'column',
```

```
}, {
    name: 'On Linux',
    data: ['8', '15', '28', '32', '38'],
    type: 'column',
}, {
    name: 'On Mac',
    data: ['12', '20', '33', '40', '45'],
    type: 'area'
}, {
    name: 'On Others',
    data: ['2', '8', '15', '18', '22'],
    type: 'area'
}]
```

Here, the `name` attribute specifies the platform and the `data` attribute specifies the adoption percentage over the years. Notice that the first two in the series have the `type` attribute as `column` and the other two as `area`. The next step is to update the `valueAxis` option and specify the details about the axis that needs to be plotted:

```
valueAxis: [{
    title: {
        text: 'Windows'
    },
    min: 0,
    max: 60
}, {
    title: {
        text: 'Linux'
    },
    min: 0,
    max: 60
}, {
    title: {
        text: 'Mac'
    },
    min: 0,
    max: 45
}, {
    title: {
        text: 'Others'
    },
    min: 0,
    max: 45
}]
```

The `valueAxis` field specifies the axes that need to be plotted on the chart. These are defined in the same order as the ones in the `series` field. The `min` and `max` attributes are used to adjust the `valueAxes` option. In the preceding code snippet, the `min` and `max` attributes for the Windows and Linux platforms are `0` and `60`, which indicates that the *y* axis that was used to project the value will start at 0 and will go up to 60. Similarly, for the other two platforms, the *y* axis would range from 0 to 45.

When you execute the page, you will notice that there is one horizontal axis (the *x* axis), which refers to the categories (the `year` data), and four vertical axes (the *y* axis), which refer to the platforms. All the four vertical axes that refer to the platforms are plotted on the left-hand side. If you want to move some of these vertical axes to the right, then you will have to specify the `axisCrossingValues` array in the `categoryAxis` option:

```
categoryAxis: {
  categories: [2010, 2011, 2012, 2013, 2014],
  axisCrossingValues: [0, 0, 5, 5]
}
```

Here, the `axisCrossingValues` field is used to specify the crossing value for each axis. The values in the array are used to indicate the indices for each series. A zero value indicates that the axis is aligned on the left-hand side (no changes); any other value would indicate its position from the left. In the previous example, the value `five` is used to move the axis to the right-hand side, since the indices zero to four are used by the categories `2010` to `2014`.

How it works...

When you execute the page without specifying the `axisCrossingValues` field, the various axes are plotted on the left-hand side, shown as follows:

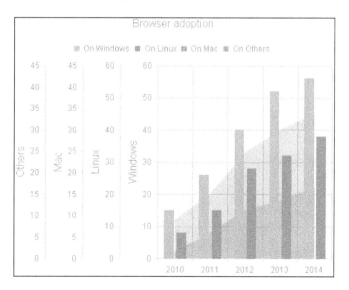

Here, the library starts plotting the vertical axes in the order in which they are defined in the `series` field, moving towards the left. After specifying the `axisCrossingValues` field, the axis for the **Mac** and **Others** series would be moved to the right-hand side, as shown in the following screenshot:

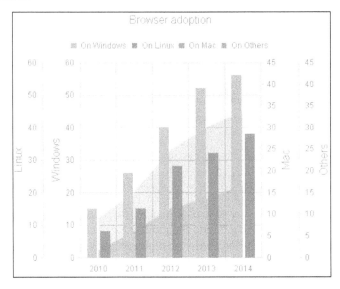

There's more...

When working with a multiaxis chart, a series can be turned off by clicking on its legend. For example, when you click on the **On Windows** legend, the corresponding series would be hidden.

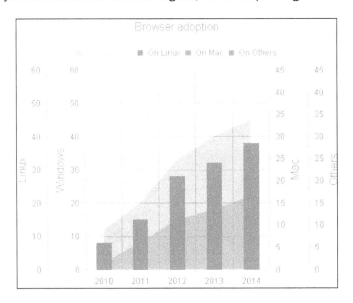

Notice that in the preceding screenshot, the **On Windows** legend is grayed out and the corresponding series is hidden from the chart. This enables users or consumers of the application to look through various series and compare them, as required.

Displaying data over a period of time and using aggregate functions

When you work on a data analytics project, you usually come across use cases of plotting a chart, which displays some data over a period of time. For example, in an order-management system, you would like to display the order data and plot it against a period of time. This period could be for a day, week, month, or year. Also, you would like to display data in terms of, say, the average bill value, number of orders, or total business made during the specified period of time.

The Kendo chart library allows you to project the data based on the given period and also apply some of the aggregate functions when displaying this data.

How to do it...

Let's first consider an example dataset that contains the order data:

```
var orderStats = [{
        billAmount: 80,
        date: new Date('2014/01/01')
    }, {
        billAmount: 95,
        date: new Date('2014/01/01')
    }, {
        billAmount: 100,
        date: new Date('2014/01/01')
    }, {
        billAmount: 85,
        date: new Date('2014/01/01')
    }, {
        billAmount: 120,
        date: new Date('2014/01/02')
    }, {
        billAmount: 130,
        date: new Date('2014/01/02')
    }, {
        billAmount: 100,
```

```
        date: new Date('2014/01/02')
    },
      .
      .
    . {
        billAmount: 80,
        date: new Date('2014/01/07')
    }, {
        billAmount: 70,
        date: new Date('2014/01/07')
    }
  ]
```

In the `DataSource` object mentioned in the preceding code snippet, each order contains two fields, namely `billAmount` and `date`. The order data spans from January 1, 2014 to January 7, 2014. This is only an example data and you can consider the data that spans over a month or a year.

There are two levels at which we want to display analytics:

▶ Data over a period of time

▶ Data that is grouped by date and on which some of the aggregate functions, such as average, total, and count, are applied

To display data over a period of time, you can set the `baseUnit` value in the `categoryAxis` field:

```
categoryAxis: {
  baseUnit: 'days'
}
```

This will group the objects in the `DataSource` object by days. The other possible options are weeks, months, and years. The `aggregate` field is to specify the aggregate function to be used in the series, as shown in the following code snippet:

```
series: [{
    type: 'area',
    aggregate: 'sum',
    field: 'billAmount',
    categoryField: 'date',
    labels: {
        visible: true,
        background: 'transparent'
    },
    color: '#0F0'
}]
```

Here, in the `series` definition, the `aggregate` field specifies `sum` as the aggregate function to be used; this means that the chart will plot the total business made by a restaurant over a period of time. The other possible values that can be assigned to the aggregate include `avg`, `count`, `first`, `min`, and `max`. There is also an option to provide a `custom` aggregator function, which would return a value that should be used to project the data.

> The `series` option specifies the color for the series and the `labels` option is used to display the data value on the chart. When you display a single series, all options can be specified in the `series` option instead of using the `seriesDefaults` option.

How it works...

When you execute the page, the order data is plotted on the chart, showing the total business made over a period of days, as shown in the following screenshot:

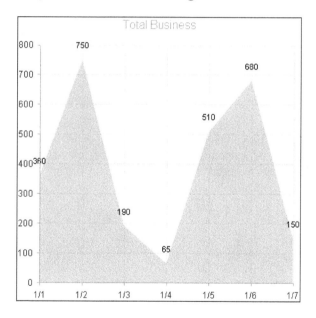

Similarly, you can create multiple charts that use the other aggregate functions, such as `avg` and `count`, to display the average bill value and the total number of orders made over a period of time, respectively.

You can build a dashboard showing these statistics by creating multiple `div` elements on the page (one for each chart), plotting data grouped by dates, and using aggregate functions.

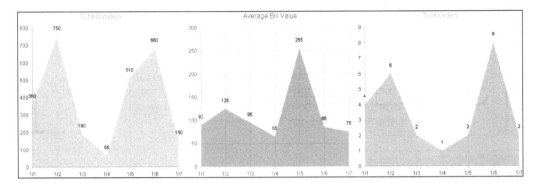

There's more...

The area charts that were built in the previous example connected the values by a straight line. You can customize this by specifying the style of line to be used. The possible values are `step` and `smooth`:

```
line: {
    style: 'smooth'
}
```

When you specify `smooth`, the values in the chart are connected by a smooth line, that is, a curved line that connects the two points such that the chart looks like a curved line drawn to connect all the points, shown as follows:

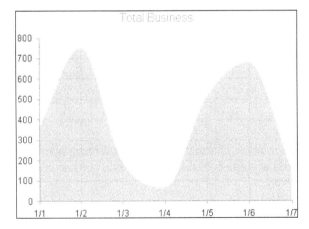

When you specify the style of the line as `step`, the values on the chart are connected by a line at right angles.

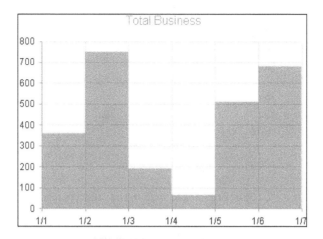

Making a chart interactive by adding events

The Kendo UI Chart library can define various event handlers, which will be triggered when the user hovers or clicks on a data item in a series. In this recipe, we will display a tooltip when the user hovers over a data item in the chart, and in another example, we will change the color of the selected column when the user clicks on it.

How to do it...

Let's consider the same `DataSource` object that we used to show the adoption of the Chrome browser over the years. In this example, let's add another field, `feature`, that we will use to show `tooltip`:

```
var chromeBrowser = [{
  'year'       : 2008,
  'percentage' : 0,
  'feature'    : 'First stable release'
}, {
  'year'       : 2009,
  'percentage' : 4,
  'feature'    : 'HTML5 Video and Audio tag support'
}, {
  'year'       : 2010,
  'percentage' : 15,
  'feature'    : 'Support for WebM videos'
}, {
  'year'       : 2011,
  'percentage' : 26,
  'feature'    : 'Hardware accelerated 3D CSS'
```

```
}, {
    'year'        : 2012,
    'percentage'  : 40,
    'feature'     : 'New Extensions API'
}, {
    'year'        : 2013,
    'percentage'  : 52,
    'feature'     : 'Web Speech API'
}, {
    'year'        : 2014,
    'percentage'  : 56,
    'feature'     : 'Different look for Win8 metro mode'
}];
```

The next step is to specify the `tooltip` option that contains fields that will be used to display a tooltip when the user hovers over a data item in the series, using the following code snippet:

```
tooltip: {
    visible: true,
    template: '#= dataItem.feature #',
    background: '#0F0'
}
```

Here, the template field contains the `dataIteam.feature` value. The `dataItem` field refers to the object that is used to plot the column in the chart. The other possible values include `category`, which refers to the category in `categoryAxis`, which, in this case, would be the `year` field; `value`, which refers to the percentage value used to draw the column; and `series`, which refers to the entire series object.

To handle click events, specify the `seriesClick` option:

```
seriesClick: function (e) {
    //iterate over series data and set the color for each series
    for (vari = 0, j = e.series.data.length; i < j; i++) {
        e.series.data[i].color = '#00F';
    }
    //change the color of the selected series
    e.dataItem.color = '#F00';
    //redraw the graph - required for the changes to get reflected
    this.redraw();
}
```

The first statement in the preceding function loops through all the objects in the series and resets the color; then, the selected item in the series is assigned a different color. The chart needs to be refreshed or redrawn to bring these changes into effect; hence, the last line invokes the redraw function on this. The `this` object refers to the context; in this case, this is the series object.

The other way to subscribe to the event is to add a listener using the `bind` method on the chart object:

```
var chart = $('#chart').data('kendoChart');
chart.bind('seriesClick', function (e) {
    for (vari = 0, j = e.series.data.length; i < j; i++) {
        e.series.data[i].color = '#00F';
    }
    e.dataItem.color = '#F00';
    this.redraw();
});
```

The first line in the preceding code snippet gets a reference to the chart object. The `chart` object is then used to subscribe to the `seriesClick` event. Now when the user clicks on a particular column in the series, the callback function will be invoked.

 When the chart is refreshed or redrawn, an animation is shown while the chart is drawn. To disable the animation, specify the `transitions` property as `false`.

How it works...

When you hover over the plotted area, you will see that the `feature` value in the data item is shown as a tooltip, as shown in the following screenshot:

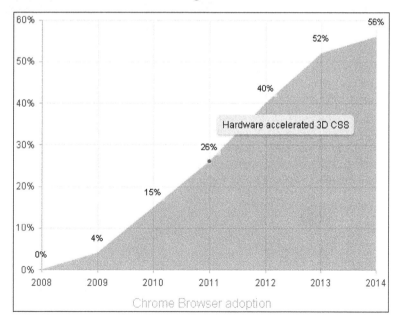

Now change the series type to `column` and refresh the page; you will see that all columns in the chart are of the same color. When you click on any column in the chart, the selected column's color is changed and redrawn.

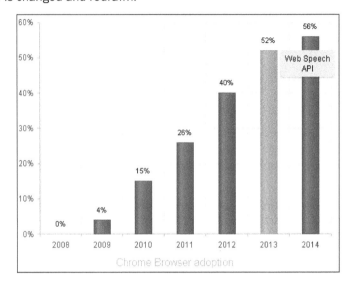

In the preceding screenshot, the selected column's color has changed and is highlighted in the chart.

Changing the chart type dynamically

In this recipe, we will take a look at how the type and skin of the chart can be changed at runtime. For example, if you have projected a column chart and you want to change it to, say, a line chart, then changes can be made to the series and the chart will be updated. This is useful in cases where you would like to visually represent data in various forms but you can't because of the space constraint. In this recipe, we will construct the chart using the `data` attributes instead of using the `kendoChart` function. This is another way of constructing a chart. Also, we will use the Model View ViewModel pattern to make changes to the chart when the user changes its type or skin. This pattern obliterates the use of adding event handlers and, instead, relies on listening to model changes to update the chart dynamically.

How to do it...

Let's create a chart by specifying various options as data attributes:

```
<div id="chartArea" data-role="chart" data-title="{text: 'Browser
    adoption', position: 'bottom'}" data-category-axis="{field:
    'year'}" data-series-defaults="{type: 'area'}" data-
    theme="blueopal" data-legend="{position: 'bottom'}" data-
    series="[
```

```
{ field: 'chrome', name: 'Chrome' },
{ field: 'firefox', name: 'Firefox'},
{ field: 'safari', name: 'Safari'},
{ field: 'ie', name: 'IE' }
]" data-bind="{source: dataSet}" style="width: 500px; height:
  400px">
</div>
```

In the preceding code snippet, all the options are specified as `data` attributes. The `data` attribute role, with its value set to `chart`, will initialize the `div` element as a `chart` widget. It also has the `data-bind` attribute, which specifies its `source` as `dataset`. The `data-bind` attribute is used to specify the model-binding values. In this case, the source binding, that is, the `DataSource` object to which this chart is bound, is specified. The `ViewModel` object that we will construct soon will specify a `dataset` attribute.

The next step is to create two dropdowns, one that lists the chart types and the other that lists the various themes or skins that should be applied. Let's also add a checkbox that represents whether the chart should be stacked or not, as shown in the following code snippet:

```
<select id="chartTypeDropdown" data-bind="value: chartType,
events: {change: onChangeHandler}">
    <option value="area">Area</option>
    <option value="line">Line</option>
    <option value="column">Column</option>
</select>
<select id="chartSkin" data-bind="value: chartSkin,
events: {change: onChangeHandler}">
    <option value="default">Default</option>
    <option value="blueopal">BlueOpal</option>
    <option value="bootstrap">Bootstrap</option>
    <option value="highcontrast">HighContrast</option>
    <option value="metro">Metro</option>
    <option value="metroblack">MetroBlack</option>
    <option value="silver">Silver</option>
    <option value="uniform">Uniform</option>
</select>
<input type="checkbox" data-bind="checked: isStacked,
events: {change: onChangeHandler}" />Stacked
```

Here, the `select` elements and the `input` element has the `data-bind` attribute specified. This attribute specifies the model binding for `value` and `checked`, respectively and also specifies the event binding for the `change` event. All these should be specified in `ViewModel`.

The next step is to specify the data source that will be used to plot the chart. Let's use the same data source that we used in earlier recipes:

```
var browserAdoption = [{
    'year': 2011,
    'chrome': 40,
    'firefox': 30,
    'ie': 15,
    'safari': 15
}, {
    'year': 2012,
    'chrome': 45,
    'firefox': 25,
    'ie': 12,
    'safari': 18
}, {
    'year': 2013,
    'chrome': 50,
    'firefox': 22,
    'ie': 8,
    'safari': 20
}];
```

The final step is to create a `ViewModel` object that contains all the model attributes that will be consumed by the previously mentioned elements. It should also specify the `onChangeHandler` function, which will be called when the user changes the values in the dropdown or selects the `stacked` checkbox, as shown in the following code snippet:

```
var viewModel = kendo.observable({
    chartType: 'area',
    chartSkin: 'blueopal',
    isStacked: false,
    onChangeHandler: function (e) {
        var chart = $('#chartArea').data('kendoChart');
        chart.setOptions({
            seriesDefaults: {
                type: this.chartType,
                stack: this.isStacked
            },
            theme: this.chartSkin
        });
```

```
        chart.refresh();
    },
    dataSet: new kendo.data.DataSource({
        data: browserAdoption
    })
});
```

Here, the bindings for various model attributes such as `chartType`, `chartSkin`, `isStacked`, `dataset`, and `onChangeHandler` are specified. The `onChangeHandler` function is an event handler that handles change events from dropdowns and the input checkbox. When one of these values change, the chart will be updated. The `setOptions` function is used to specify the type and stack value in the `seriesDefaults` field and also the theme to be used for the chart. The `refresh` function is then called to update the chart. The `dataSet` attribute specifies the `DataSource` object to be used when plotting the chart.

How it works...

When you render the page, you will see an **area** chart with the **BlueOpal** skin applied to it, as shown in the following screenshot:

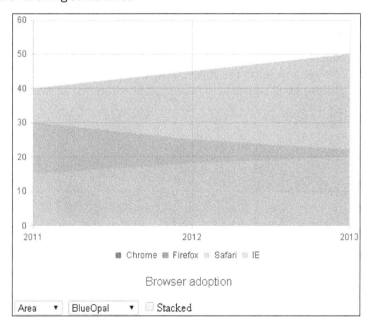

Now, let's change the type of chart to **Line** and the theme to **Silver**; this will trigger the onChangeHandler function in the ViewModel object and the chart will be updated with the selected options.

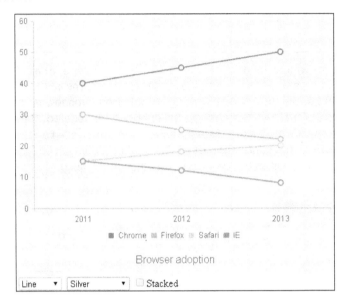

Now, let's change all three options, that is, type to **Column**, theme to **Bootstrap**, and select the **Stacked** option. When you select the checkbox, the stack option is set to true and the series data will now be stacked instead of showing four different columns for each browser.

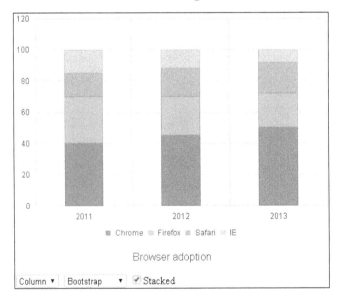

In the preceding screenshot, the values for various series are stacked one above the other.

11
Kendo UI DataViz – Advance Charting

In this chapter, we will cover the following recipes:

- ▸ Creating a chart to show stock history
- ▸ Using the Radial Gauge widget
- ▸ Using the Linear Gauge widget
- ▸ Generating barcode images using various encoding methods
- ▸ Generating a QR code image to represent a URL, e-mail, telephone, and geographic location
- ▸ Creating flow diagrams using Kendo Diagram
- ▸ Creating hierarchical structural diagrams using `layouts`
- ▸ Creating a map to display geospatial information using an `OpenStreet` map
- ▸ Creating a map by binding it to the `GeoJSON` data

Introduction

The Kendo UI library provides several advance charting widgets that can be used to visualize data. These include the Stock Chart widget that shows you the stock price history of a particular stock, the Map widget that visualizes data on a map, the Gauge widget that creates a dashboard that contains gauge charts, Barcode and QRCode widgets that allow you to create codes that can be used to identify products, and the Diagram widget that creates diagrams that show you nested relationships between various entities. These are some of the advance charts in addition to the basic charts mentioned in the previous chapter.

Creating a chart to show stock history

The Kendo UI library provides a specialized chart widget that can be used to display the stock price data for a particular stock over a period of time. In this recipe, we will take a look at creating a Stock chart and customizing it.

Getting started

Include the CSS files, `kendo.dataviz.min.css` and `kendo.dataviz.default.min.css`, in the `head` section. These files are used in styling some of the parts of a stock history chart.

How to do it...

A Stock chart is made up of two charts: a pane that shows you the stock history and another pane that is used to navigate through the chart by changing the date range.

The stock price for a particular stock on a day can be denoted by the following five attributes:

- ▸ `Open`: This shows you the value of the stock when the trading starts for the day
- ▸ `Close`: This shows you the value of the stock when the trading closes for the day
- ▸ `High`: This shows you the highest value the stock was able to attain on the day
- ▸ `Low`: This shows you the lowest value the stock reached on the day
- ▸ `Volume`: This shows you the total number of shares of that stock traded on the day

Let's assume that a service returns this data in the following format:

```
[
    {
    "Date"  : "2013/01/01",
    "Open"  : 40.11,
    "Close" : 42.34,
    "High"  : 42.5,
    "Low"   : 39.5,
    "Volume": 10000
    }
    .
    .
    .
]
```

We will use the preceding data to create a Stock chart. The `kendoStockChart` function is used to create a Stock chart, and it is configured with a set of options similar to the area chart or Column chart, as mentioned in the previous chapter. In addition to the `series` data, you can specify the `navigator` option to show a navigation pane below the chart that contains the entire stock history:

```
$("#chart").kendoStockChart({
  title: {
    text: 'Stock history'
  },

  dataSource: {
    transport: {
      read: '/services/stock?q=ADBE'
    }
  },

  dateField: "Date",

  series: [{
    type: "candlestick",
    openField: "Open",
    closeField: "Close",
    highField: "High",
    lowField: "Low"
  }],

  navigator: {
    series: {
      type: 'area',
      field: 'Volume'
    }
  }
});
```

In the preceding code snippet, the `DataSource` object refers to the remote service that would return the stock data for a set of days. The `series` option specifies the series type as `candlestick`; a candlestick chart is used here to indicate the stock price for a particular day. The mappings for `openField`, `closeField`, `highField`, and `lowField` are specified; they will be used in plotting the chart and also to show a tooltip when the user hovers over it. The `navigator` option is specified to create an area chart, which uses volume data to plot the chart. The `dateField` option is used to specify the mapping between the date fields in the chart and the one in the response.

How it works...

When you load the page, you will see two panes being shown; the navigator is below the main chart. By default, the chart displays data for all the dates in the `DataSource` object, as shown in the following screenshot:

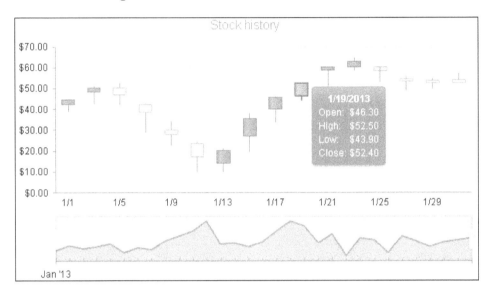

In the preceding screenshot, a candlestick chart is created and it shows you the stock price over a period of time. Also, notice that in the navigator pane, all date ranges are selected by default, and hence, they are reflected in the chart (candlestick) as well. When you hover over the series, you will notice that the stock quote for the selected date is shown. This includes the date and other fields such as **Open**, **High**, **Low**, and **Close**.

The area of the chart is adjusted to show you the stock price for various dates such that the dates are evenly distributed. In the previous case, the dates range from January 1, 2013 to January 31, 2013. However, when you hover over the series, you will notice that some of the dates are omitted. To overcome this, you can either increase the width of the chart area or use the navigator to reduce the date range. The former option is not advisable if the date range spans across several months and years.

To reduce the date range in the navigator, move the two date range selectors towards each other to narrow down the dates, as shown in the following screenshot:

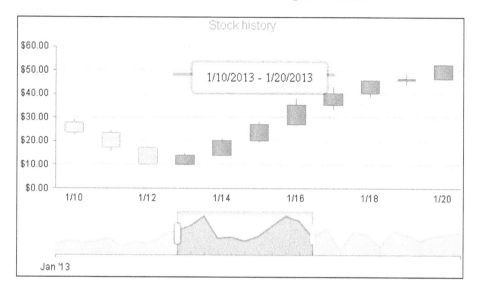

When you try to narrow down the dates, you will see a tooltip in the chart, indicating the date range that you are trying to select. The candlestick chart is adjusted to show you the stock price for the selected date range. Also, notice that the opacity of the selected date range in the navigator remains the same while the rest of the area's opacity is reduced. Once the date range is selected, the selected pane can be moved in the navigator.

There's more...

There are several options available to you to customize the behavior and the look and feel of the Stock Chart widget.

Specifying the date range in the navigator when initializing the chart

By default, all date ranges in the chart are selected and the user will have to narrow them down in the navigator pane. When you work with a large dataset, you will want to show the stock data for a specific range of date when the chart is rendered. To do this, specify the `select` option in `navigator`:

```
navigator: {
  series: {
    type: 'area',
```

```
      field: 'Volume'
    },
    select: {
      from: '2013/01/07',
      to: '2013/01/14'
    }
  }
}
```

In the previous code snippet, the from and to date ranges are specified. Now, when you render the page, you will see that the same dates are selected in the navigator pane.

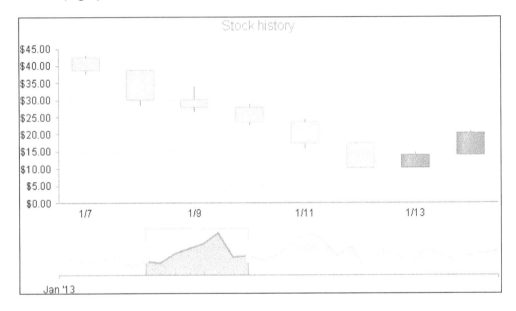

Customizing the look and feel of the Stock Chart widget

There are various options available to customize the navigator pane in the Stock Chart widget. Let's increase the height of the pane and also include a title text for it:

```
navigator: {

  .

  .

  pane: {
    height: '50px',
    title: {
      text: 'Stock Volume'
    }
  }
}
```

Now when you render the page, you will see that the title and height of the navigator pane has been increased.

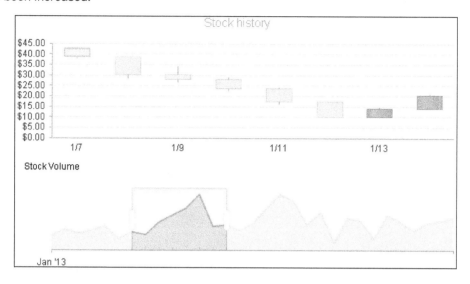

Using the Radial Gauge widget

The Radial Gauge widget allows you to build a dashboard-like application wherein you want to indicate a value that lies in a specific range. For example, a car's dashboard can contain a couple of Radial Gauge widgets that can be used to indicate the current speed and RPM.

How to do it...

To create a Radial Gauge widget, invoke the `kendoRadialGauge` function on the selected DOM element. A Radial Gauge widget contains some components, and it can be configured by providing options, as shown in the following code snippet:

```
$("#chart").kendoRadialGauge({

  scale: {
    startAngle: 0,
    endAngle: 180,
    min: 0,
    max: 180
  },
  pointer: {
    value: 20
  }
});
```

Here the scale option is used to configure the range for the Radial Gauge widget. The `startAngle` and `endAngle` options are used to indicate the angle at which the Radial Gauge widget's range should start and end. By default, its values are 30 and 210, respectively. The other two options, that is, `min` and `max`, are used to indicate the range values over which the value can be plotted. The `pointer` option is used to indicate the current value in the Radial Gauge widget.

There are several options available to configure the Radial Gauge widget; these include positioning of the labels and configuring the look and feel of the widget.

How it works...

When you render the page, you will see a Radial Gauge widget that shows you the scale from **0** to **180** and the pointer pointing to the value **20**.

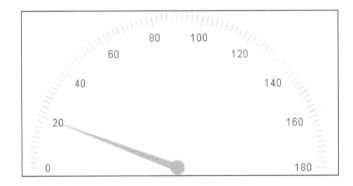

Here, the values from **0** to **180** are evenly distributed, that is, the major ticks are in terms of **20**. There are 10 minor ticks, that is, ticks between two major ticks. The widget shows values in the clockwise direction. Also, the pointer value **20** is selected in the scale.

There's more...

The Radial Gauge widget can be customized to a great extent by including various options when initializing the widget.

Changing the major and minor unit values

Specify the `majorUnit` and `minorUnit` options in the scale:

```
scale: {
   startAngle: 0,
   endAngle: 180,
```

```
    min: 0,
    max: 180,
    majorUnit: 30,
    minorUnit: 10,
}
```

The `scale` option specifies the `majorUnit` value as `30` (instead of the default 20) and `minorUnit` as `10`. This will now add labels at every 30 units and show you two minor ticks between the two major ticks, each at a distance of 10 units, as shown in the following screenshot:

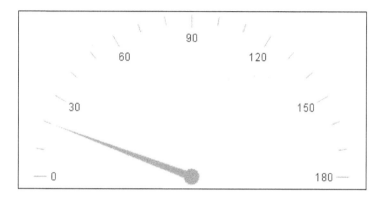

The ticks shown in the preceding screenshot can also be customized:

```
    scale: {
        .
        .
        minorTicks: {
            size: 30,
            width: 1,
            color: 'green'
        },
        majorTicks: {
            size: 100,
            width: 2,
            color: 'red'
        }
    }
```

Here, the `size` option is used to specify the length of the tick marker, `width` is used to specify the thickness of the tick, and the `color` option is used to change the color of the tick.

Now when you render the page, you will see the changes for the major and minor ticks.

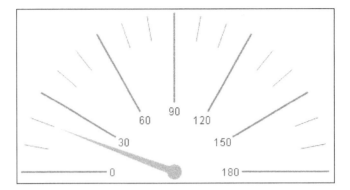

Changing the color of the radial using the ranges option

The `scale` attribute can include the `ranges` option to specify a radial color for the various ranges on the Radial Gauge widget:

```
scale: {
    .

    .

    ranges: [
        {
            from: 0,
            to: 60,
            color: '#00F'
        }, {
            from: 60,
            to: 130,
            color: '#0F0'
        }, {
            from: 130,
            to: 200,
            color: '#F00'
        }
    ]
}
```

In the preceding code snippet, the `ranges` array contains three objects that specify the color to be applied on the circumference of the widget. The `from` and `to` values are used to specify the range of tick values for which the color should be applied.

Now when you render the page, you will see the Radial Gauge widget showing the colors for various ranges along the circumference of the widget, as shown in the following screenshot:

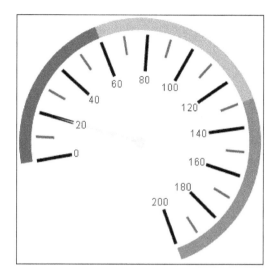

In the preceding screenshot, the startAngle and endAngle fields are changed to 10 and 250, respectively. The widget can be further customized by moving the labels outside. This can be done by specifying the labels attribute with position as outside.

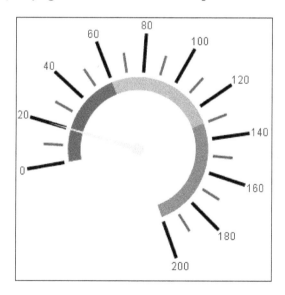

In the preceding screenshot, the labels are positioned outside, hence, the radial appears inside.

Updating the pointer value using a Slider widget

The `pointer` value is set when the Radial Gauge widget is initialized. It is possible to change the `pointer` value of the widget at runtime using a Slider widget. The changes in the Slider widget can be observed, and the `pointer` value of the Radial Gauge can be updated accordingly.

Let's use the same Radial Gauge widget mentioned in the previous recipe. A Slider widget is created using an input element:

```
<input id="slider" value="0" />
```

The next step is to initialize the previously mentioned input element to a Slider widget:

```
$('#slider').kendoSlider({
    min: 0,
    max: 200,
    showButtons: false,
    smallStep: 10,
    tickPlacement: 'none',
    change: updateRadialGuage
});
```

The `min` and `max` values specify the range of values that can be set for the slider. The `smallStep` attribute specifies the minimum increment value of the slider. The `change` attribute specifies the function that should be invoked when the `slider` value changes.

The `updateRadialGuage` function should then update the value of the pointer in the Radial Gauge widget:

```
function updateRadialGuage() {
    $('#chart').data('kendoRadialGauge')
            .value($('#slider').val());
}
```

The function gets the instance of the widget and then sets its value to the value obtained from the Slider widget.

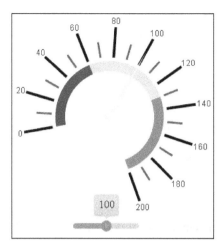

Here, the `slider` value is changed to `100`, and you will notice that it is reflected in the Radial Gauge widget.

Using the Linear Gauge widget

The Linear Gauge widget is also used to indicate where a value lies in the given range. It is similar to the Radial Gauge widget and takes the same set of options as well. It is used to display the value on a linear scale.

How to do it...

Linear Gauge is created by invoking the `kendoLinearGauge` function on the DOM element. It uses the same options as the Radial Gauge widget:

```
$("#chart").kendoLinearGauge({

    pointer: {
      value: 20,
    },

    scale: {
      min: 0,
```

```
        max: 200,
        majorUnit: 20,
        minorUnit: 10
    }

});
```

This will display the Linear Gauge widget with its pointer at **20**. By default, the widget is displayed vertically, that is, the value is projected on the *y* axis. To display the widget horizontally, specify `vertical` as `false` under the `scale` option. This will display the widget horizontally.

How it works...

When you render the page, the Linear Gauge is displayed vertically, as shown in the following screenshot:

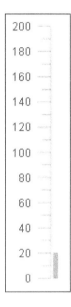

After setting `vertical` as `false`, the widget is displayed horizontally.

As with the Radial Gauge, the Linear Gauge can also include the `ranges` option. After including the `ranges` option, you will see the widget showing this option along its scale.

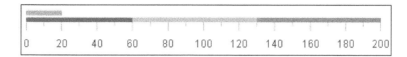

The pointer shown on the Linear Gauge is `barIndicator` by default. The other option available is `arrow`. To change the pointer, set `shape` to `arrow` under the `pointer` option:

```
pointer: {
  value: 20,
  shape: 'arrow'
}
```

Now when you render the page, you will see an arrow.

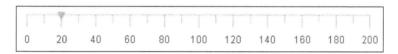

Generating barcode images using various encoding methods

The Kendo UI library provides APIs that can be used to generate the barcode graphic image for the given value. For example, each product in the supermarket can have a barcode associated with it. When a customer purchases the product, the barcode would be used to get the product price and other details. The library can generate the barcode by referring to the unique identifier.

How to do it...

A barcode image can be generated by invoking the `kendoBarcode` function on the DOM element:

```
$("#chart").kendoBarcode({
  value: '1234567'
});
```

Here, the `1234567` value will be encoded using the default encoding, that is, `code39`. You can also specify the encoding method to be used by specifying the `type` field:

```
$("#chart").kendoBarcode({
  value: '1234567',
  type: 'ean8'
});
```

In the preceding code snippet, the encoding type is set to `ean8`. The other possible values are `EAN13`, `UPCE`, `UPCA`, `Code11`, `Code39`, `Code39Extended`, `Code93`, `Code93Extended`, `Code128`, `Code128A`, `Code128B`, `Code128C`, `GS1-128`, `MSImod10`, `MSImod11`, `MSImod1010`, `MSImod1100`, and `POSTNET`. The `value` attribute is mandatory and a barcode is generated using the value and the specified encoding type.

How it works...

When you don't specify the encoding type, the `code39` encoding is used to generate the barcode, as shown in the following screenshot:

The value is shown in the previous barcode. To hide the value, specify the `text` attribute and set the `visible` option to false:

```
$("#chart").kendoBarcode({
  value: '1234567',
  text: {
    visible: false
  }
});
```

When you use some other encoding type, for example, `ean8`, the barcode is generated accordingly.

Generating a QR code image to represent a URL, e-mail, telephone, and geographic location

A **Quick Response code** (**QR code**) is generally used to efficiently store data by encoding it. It uses ISO_8859_1 as the encoding method by default to store data. The generated code consists of black modules (square dots) arranged in a square grid on a white background. This code can then be read by a camera and then processed by an application.

In this recipe, we will see how various forms of data such as URLs, e-mail addresses, telephone numbers, and geographic locations can be stored in a QR code.

How to do it...

To generate a QR code, invoke the `kendoQRCode` function on the DOM element:

```
$("#chart").kendoQRCode({
  value: 'http://www.kendoui.com'
});
```

In the previous example, the `http://www.kendoui.com` URL is specified. This value will be encoded using ISO_8859_1 and represented in a square grid. When you scan the QR code, the value stored in it is identified. Since the value is prefixed with the protocol name, `http://`, the value is recognized as a URL. Similarly, an e-mail address should be prefixed with `mailto:`, a telephone number with `tel`, and a geolocation with `geo` followed by the latitude and longitude information. A geo location can be encoded in the following way:

```
$("#chart").kendoQRCode({
  value: 'geo: 12.9667, 77.5667, 100'
});
```

By default, the color of the QR code is black and is drawn on a white background. This can be changed by specifying the `color` and `background` attributes:

```
$("#chart").kendoQRCode({
  value: 'geo: 12.9667, 77.5667, 100',
  color: 'red',
  background: 'yellow'
});
```

How it works...

When you render the page, you will see a square grid that shows you the dots and lines that represent the QR code for the URL.

When you change the value to the geolocation and specify the `color` and `background` attributes, the generated QR code is shown as follows:

There's more...

A QR code has an error correction capability that allows you to restore data if the code is damaged or is dirty. There are four error correction levels, namely, L, M, Q, and H, that can be applied to a QR code. Each of these levels indicate the percentage of data that can be recovered, that is, L recovers 7 percent data, M recovers 15 percent, Q recovers 25 percent data, and H recovers 30 percent. When initializing a QR code, one can change the error correction level by setting the `errorCorrection` attribute:

```
$("#chart").kendoQRCode({
    value: 'geo: 12.9667, 77.5667, 100',
    errorCorrection: 'Q'
});
```

In the previous example, the `errorCorrection` attribute is set to Q, and it is used to encode the value.

Creating flow diagrams using Kendo Diagram

Adding workflow diagrams or hierarchical structure to a web page is now made easy with the introduction of diagrams in the Kendo UI library. In this recipe, we will build a flowchart diagram by creating shapes and then we will connect those with connectors. The library also provides a set of layouts that can be used to represent a hierarchical or tree-like structure.

How to do it...

A flowchart is used to represent steps in an algorithm; these steps are shown as shapes (rectangles and circles). The connectors are then used to connect the shapes and describe the flow. A diagram in Kendo UI is created by invoking the `kendoDiagram` function on the selected DOM node:

```
var diagram = $("#chart").kendoDiagram({

  connectionDefaults: {
    stroke: {
      color: '#F00'
    },
    startCap: 'FilledCircle',
    endCap: 'ArrowEnd',
  }

}).getKendoDiagram();
```

In the preceding code snippet, an empty diagram is created, with some default attributes for connections specified. A connection is used to connect two or more shapes in the diagram. The `connectionDefaults` option specifies the color of the stroke to be applied; the `startCap` and `endCap` options are used to specify the decoration to be applied. In this case, the `startCap` option has the value `FilledCircle`, which will show you a circle at the start of the connection. The other value that can be assigned to `startCap` is `ArrowStart`. This will add an arrow directed towards the shape. The `endCap` option has its value set to `ArrowEnd`. In this example, the shape from which the connection is initiated will have a filled circle attached to it, and an arrow is shown, which is directed towards the second shape.

The `getKendoDiagram` function will return an instance of the diagram once it's initialized. The diagram is like a canvas on which you can add several shapes and also connect them.

Now let's create a function that will accept the shape details, which includes the text that needs to be shown, the shape type, and the position of the shape on the diagram:

```
function createShape(textData, type, positionX, positionY) {

    return new kendo.dataviz.diagram.Shape({
        x: positionX,
        y: positionY,
        width: 100,
        height: 50,
        type: type,
        content: {
            text: textData,
            color: '#FFF'
        },
        background: '#00B'
    });

}
```

In the preceding code snippet, the `createShape` function accepts the mentioned arguments and returns an instance of `shape`, that is, `kendo.dataviz.diagram.Shape`. Now let's create a few shapes and add them to the diagram:

```
var shape1 = diagram.addShape(
                    createShape('Start', 'circle', 400, 20));
var shape2 = diagram.addShape(
                    createShape('counter = 0', 'rectangle' , 400,
    100));
var shape3 = diagram.addShape(
                    createShape('counter < 5', 'rectangle', 400,
    190));
var shape4 = diagram.addShape(
                    createShape('Stop', 'circle', 600, 290));
var shape5 = diagram.addShape(
                    createShape('Print (counter)', 'rectangle',
    200, 290));
var shape6 = diagram.addShape(
                    createShape('counter++', 'rectangle', 200,
    390));
```

In the preceding code snippet, six shape objects are created by specifying their content text along with the position data. There are two types of shapes that you can create, rectangles and circles. Once the shapes have been created, they are added to the diagram by calling the addShape function on the diagram object.

Once the shapes have been added, connections between them can be established:

```
diagram.connect(shape1, shape2);
diagram.connect(shape2, shape3);
diagram.connect(shape3.getConnector('Right'),
                shape4.getConnector('Top'), {
    points: [
      new kendo.dataviz.diagram.Point(650, 215)
    ]
});
diagram.connect(shape3.getConnector('Left'),
                shape5.getConnector('Top'), {
    points: [
      new kendo.dataviz.diagram.Point(250, 215)
    ]
});
diagram.connect(shape5, shape6);
diagram.connect(shape6.getConnector('Bottom'),
                shape3.getConnector('Bottom'), {
    points:[
      new kendo.dataviz.diagram.Point(250, 470),
      new kendo.dataviz.diagram.Point(450, 470)
    ]
});
```

The connect function accepts two shape objects and an optional configuration object. A connection between the two shapes is added; there are four connector points available on a shape instance, namely, Top, Bottom, Right, and Left. The framework identifies the position of the shapes on the diagram and chooses the correct connector point from the Shape instance. In the preceding example, shape2 is positioned right below shape1, and hence, the connection between the two will be from the shape1 bottom connector point to the shape2 top connector point.

In the third example, the connector point to be used is explicitly mentioned by calling shape3.getConnector('Right') and shape4.getConnector('Top'). Also, the third parameter is the configuration object that is used to configure the connector. The third parameter in the preceding code snippet specifies the points configuration. This is used to set intermediate points of the connection. This will be applied in addition to connectionDefaults, which is specified when initializing the widget.

How it works...

When you don't specify the connector, that is, when you use `diagram.connect(shape1, shape2)`, the framework determines the connector to be used and adds a connection, as shown in the following screenshot:

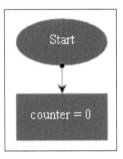

In the preceding case, `shape2` is positioned below `shape1` and appropriate connectors from the shapes are selected. When the second shape is positioned on the right-hand side, the first shape's right connector and the second shape's left connector are used to connect the two shapes.

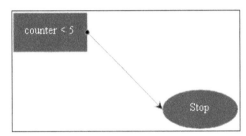

In the preceding screenshot, the line that connects the two shapes is skewed. This can be corrected by selecting the connector on each shape and adding intermediate points between the two shapes, that is, a third parameter that specifies the array of point objects.

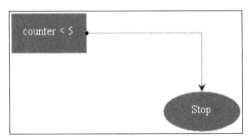

Once all the connections are added, a flowchart diagram that connects various shapes is created.

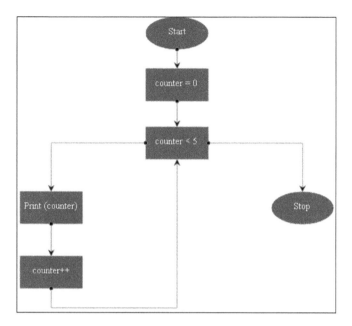

Notice that the connection between the shape with the **counter++** and **counter<5** text has two intermediate points. The `points` array is used to specify various intermediate point objects that should be used when adding a connection.

Creating hierarchical structural diagrams using layouts

In this recipe, we will take a look at building hierarchical structural diagrams or tree-like diagrams using the `layout` option in `kendoDiagram`. The hierarchical structure can be represented in the JSON format, and it can be used as a `DataSource` object when building the diagram.

How to do it...

Let's create a hierarchical structure in the JSON format, which can then be used as a `DataSource` object for building the tree diagram:

```
var data = [
  {
    "designation": "CEO",
    "name": "Mitchell Johnson",
    "manages": [
      {
        "designation": "Vice President",
```

```
        "name": "Smith Cooper",
        "manages": [
          {
            "designation": "Director",
            "name": "Andrew Walker"
          },
          {
            "designation": "Director",
            "name": "Robert Thompson"
          }
        ]
      },
      {
        "designation": "Vice President",
        "name": "Harris Jones",
        "manages": [
          {
            "designation": "Director",
            "name": "Edward Collins"
          },
          {
            "designation": "Director",
            "name": "Thomas Wang"
          }
        ]
      }
    ]
  }
];
```

In the preceding code snippet, we are creating a hierarchical structure where each object contains three fields: `designation`, `name`, and `manages`. The `manages` field represents the child nodes for a particular node. Each node will show you the `name` and `designation` fields, and then connectors would be added to represent the ones mentioned in the `manages` collection.

The next step is to specify the `DataSource` object details when creating a diagram. In the `DataSource` option, you should also specify the `schema` details to let the framework know which attribute is to be considered for adding child nodes, as shown in the following code snippet:

```
$("#chart").kendoDiagram({
    dataSource: {
        data: data,
        schema: {
```

```
            model: {
                children: "manages"
            }
        }
    },
    .
    .
    .
});
```

After specifying the `DataSource` option, the next step is to specify the `layout` details. The `layout` option is used to specify the arrangement of shapes and connections in the diagram. It will parse the data and then arrange these shapes based on the specified layout type and subtype:

```
$("#chart").kendoDiagram({
    .
    .
    .
    layout: {
        type: "tree",
        subtype: "down",
        horizontalSeparation: 50,
        verticalSeparation: 50
    },
    .
    .
    .
});
```

In the `layout` option, the type is specified as `tree` and the subtype is `down`. This will create a tree structure with the root node at the top of the diagram, followed by various child nodes. The other possible values for the subtype include the following:

- ▶ `up`: In this value, the root node is at the bottom and its child nodes are added upwards, that is, the tree will be inverted
- ▶ `left`: In this value, the root node is placed on the left-hand side and its child nodes are added to the right
- ▶ `right`: In this value, the root is placed on the right-hand side and its child nodes are added to the left-hand side
- ▶ `mindmapVertical`: In this value, the root node is at the center and its child nodes are distributed equally above and below the root node
- ▶ `mindmapHorizontal`: In this value, the root node is at the center and its child nodes are distributed equally on the left and right-hand sides of the root node
- ▶ `radial`: In this value, the root node is at the center and all its child nodes are spread around it in the form of a radial
- ▶ `tipOver`: This value is similar to a tree-down subtype, wherein the direct children are arranged horizontally and the grandchildren are arranged vertically

The other two attributes, `horizontalSeparation` and `verticalSeparation`, are used to specify the distance between the two nodes that are arranged horizontally and vertically.

The next step is to create shapes for the nodes in the `DataSource` object. In this example, we will use the `shapeDefaults` option to add shapes to the diagram, as shown in the following code snippet:

```
$("#chart").kendoDiagram({
    .

    .
    shapeDefaults: {
      visual: function (data) {
        var group = new kendo.dataviz.diagram.Group();

        //create a rectangle shape
        group.append(new kendo.dataviz.diagram.Rectangle({
          width: 130,
          height: 75,
          background: '#1696d3',
          stroke: {
            width: 0
          }
        }));

        //add text 'name' inside the rectangle
        group.append(new kendo.dataviz.diagram.TextBlock({
          text: data.dataItem.name,
          x: 10,
          y: 10,
          color: '#fff'
        }));

        //add text 'designation' inside the rectangle
        group.append(new kendo.dataviz.diagram.TextBlock({
          text: data.dataItem.designation,
          x: 10,
          y: 30,
          color: '#fff'
        }));

        return group;
      }
    },
    .
});
```

Here, the `visual` attribute's value is a function that returns a `visual` element that needs to be rendered on the diagram. In our example, we will create a `visual` element that includes the `name` and `designation` properties from the model. The function first creates a group element by creating an instance of `kendo.dataviz.diagram.Group`. A `Group` attribute is an invisible `visual` element, which is used to contain and group other `visual` elements. We then create instances for `kendo.dataviz.diagram.Rectangle` and `kendo.dataviz.diagram.TextBlock` and append it to the group. The function then returns the `group` object. This function is invoked recursively and nodes are added to the diagram.

How it works...

When the `layout` subtype is down, the root node is placed at the top and the child nodes are added, growing the tree downwards, as shown in the following screenshot:

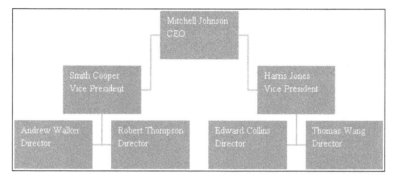

When you change the subtype to `left`, the root node is placed on the right-hand side and the nodes are added such that the tree grows from right to left.

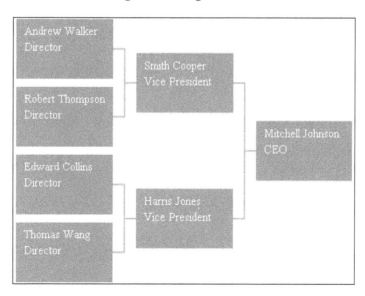

After changing the subtype to `mindmapHorizontal`, the root node is placed at the center and the child nodes are added on either side.

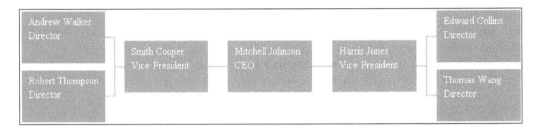

You can try changing the subtype to `radial` and `tipOver` to see the placement of nodes in the diagram.

Creating a map to display geospatial information using an OpenStreet map

The library provides APIs that you can use to display a map of a particular location on the page. In this recipe, we will create a map by using the `kendoMap` function, providing some configuration details. We will use `OpenStreet` maps to fetch images for the map.

How to do it...

To create a map, invoke the `kendoMap` function on the selected DOM node, providing the configuration options mentioned in the following code snippet:

```
$('#chart').kendoMap({
  center: [30.2681, -97.7448],
  zoom: 4,
  layers: [{
    type: 'tile',
    urlTemplate: "http://#= subdomain
#.tile2.opencyclemap.org/transport/#= zoom #/#= x #/#= y #.png",
    subdomains: ['a', 'b', 'c'],
    attribution: '&copy; <a href="http://osm.org/copyright">
      OpenStreetMap contributors</a>.' +
        'Tiles courtesy of <a href=
          "http://www.opencyclemap.org/"">Andy Allan</a>'
  }],
  .
  .
});
```

In the preceding code snippet, the `center` option is used to specify the coordinates of the map's center location. The latitude and longitude information, along with the provided map's width and height, is used to center the map in the container. The `zoom` option is used to set the zoom level of the map. The `layers` attribute is used to specify various layers that will be displayed on the map; in the previous example, the type of layer is specified as `tile`, which is used to display data from the `OpenStreet` map. The other possible values for `type` are `bing`, which is used to retrieve maps from Bing maps; `marker`, which is used to add markers to the map; and `shape`, which is used to display a vector-shape layer. These values are used when the data is bound to the `geoJSON` data. The `urlTemplate` attribute specifies the URL from which the map data has to be retrieved. It takes into account the zoom level set for the map and the *x* and *y* coordinates, that is, the latitude and longitude information specified in the `center` attribute and in the `subdomains` property. Notice that after the `urlTemplate` option, the `subdomains` property is specified. It is an array that mentions the subdomains that should be used to get map images. The browser has a limit on the number of images that can be retrieved in parallel per domain. When using `subdomains`, the images are fetched in parallel; hence, it reduces the time required to render the entire map. The `attribution` field is used to specify the attribution for the layer.

Let's now add some markers to the map. A `marker` is another layer type that can be added:

```
$('#chart').kendoMap({
    .
    .
    layers: [{
      type: 'tile',
        .
        .
    }, {
      type: 'marker',
      locationField: 'latlng ',
      tooltip: {
        content: function (e) {
          return e.sender.marker.dataItem.tooltip;
        }
      },
      dataSource: {
        data: [{
          latlng: [40.6700, -73.9400],
          tooltip: 'New York'
        }, {
          latlng: [34.0500, -118.2500],
          tooltip: 'Los Angeles'
        }]
      }
    }]
});
```

In the preceding code snippet, the type of layer is specified as `marker` and the `locationField` attribute specifies the value as `latlng`. This refers to the property in the `dataSource` option. The `dataSource` attribute specifies the marker details, that is, the latitude and longitude information where the marker must be added and the tooltip to be shown when the user hovers over the marker. The `tooltip` option contains a `content` attribute, whose value is a function that returns the tooltip information from the `dataSource` attribute.

How it works...

When you render the page, a map is shown. The map data is fetched from the specified URL, that is, from `OpenStreet` maps using various subdomains.

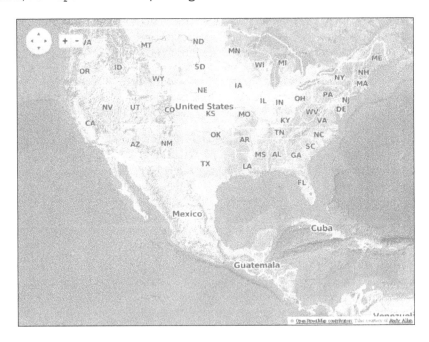

Notice that the map shows you the navigator and zoom controls at the top-left corner of the map. Also, the attribution text is shown in the bottom-right corner of the map. After adding layer markers, the map would now contain pins at the specified latitude and longitude coordinates, as shown in the following screenshot:

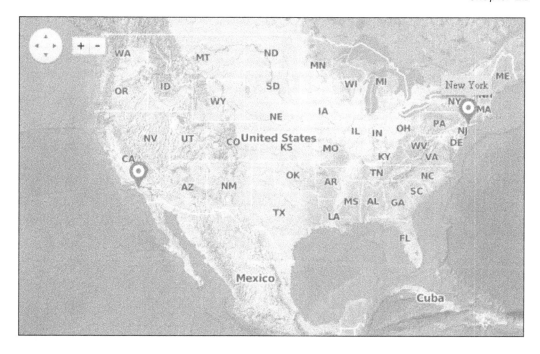

In the preceding screenshot, a tooltip is shown when the user hovers over the marker.

There's more...

In the earlier examples, the navigator, zoom, and attribution controls were placed at the top-left and at the bottom-right corners of the screen. The position of these controls can be changed by including the `controls` option and specifying the position of these controls:

```
$('#chart').kendoMap({
  .

  controls: {
    navigator: {
      position: "bottomRight"
    },
    zoom: {
      position: "bottomLeft"
    },
```

```
        attribution: {
          position: "topRight"
        }
    },
    .
});
```

Now when you render the page, the controls will be positioned accordingly.

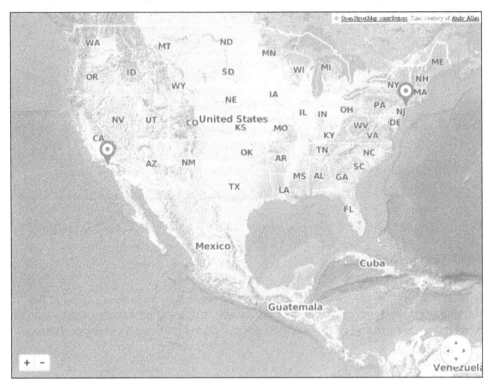

The `position` attribute can have one of the following values: `topLeft`, `topRight`, `bottomLeft`, and `bottomRight`. It is also possible to hide the controls by setting its value to `false`:

```
controls: {
    navigator: false
},
```

By setting the specified control to `false`, the control would not be shown on the page.

Creating a map by binding it to the GeoJSON data

GeoJSON is a format for encoding a variety of geographic data structures. It is an open-standard format for encoding a collection of simple geographical features along with non-spatial attributes using JSON. In this recipe, we will create a map that is bound to the geoJSON data, containing not only the coordinates, but also other non-spatial information about the area.

How to do it...

To create shapes that correspond to points or coordinates, set the `layer` type as `shape`. Let's first refer to the geoJSON data that contains the coordinates and also other non-spatial data:

```
{
    "type": "FeatureCollection",
    "features": [
        {
            "type": "Feature",
            "properties": {
                "GEO_ID": "0400000US23",
                "STATE": "23",
                "NAME": "Maine",
                "LSAD": "",
                "CENSUSAREA": 30842.923
            },
            "geometry": {
                "type": "MultiPolygon",
                "coordinates": [
                    [
                        [
                            [-67.619761, 44.519754],
                            [-67.61541, 44.521973],
                            [-67.587738, 44.516196],
                            .
                            .
                            .
                        ],
                        .
                        .
                        .
                    ]
                ]
            }
        }]
}
```

The `geoJSON` data mentioned contains the coordinates that correspond to the points on the map. These points will be used to construct vector shapes. The `geoJSON` data also lists other properties such as `NAME` and `CENSUSAREA`. Let's use the previous JSON data as a `DataSource` object in building the map using the `kendoMap` function:

```
$('#chart').kendoMap({
  center: [30.2681, -97.7448],
  zoom: 4,
  layers: [{
    type: 'shape',
    dataSource: {
      type: 'geojson',
      transport: {
        read: './geojson-us.json'
      }
    }
  }]
});
```

Here, the `type` attribute is set as `shape` and `dataSource` is specified, which refers to the file that contains the `geoJSON` data. The framework would parse the `geoJSON` data and refer to the coordinates to construct the map.

We can use other properties present in the `geoJSON` data and add some functionality to the map. For example, we could convert the `CENSUSAREA` field to a hex number and use this to fill the shape:

```
$('#chart').kendoMap({
  center: [30.2681, -97.7448],
  zoom: 4,
  layers: [{
      type: 'shape',
      dataSource: {
        type: 'geojson',
        transport: {
          read: './geojson-us.json'
        }
      }
  }],
  shapeCreated: function (e) {
    var shapeColor = parseInt(e.shape.dataItem.properties.
      CENSUSAREA, 16).toString();
    shapeColor = '#' + ('FFFFFF' + shapeColor).slice(-6);
    e.shape.fill(shapeColor);
  }
});
```

In the preceding code snippet, the `shapeCreated` function is added, which is called whenever a shape is added to the map.

How it works...

When you render the page, you will see a map created that will contain shapes, as shown in the following screenshot:

After adding colors to shapes using the `shapeCreated` function, you will see a colored map.

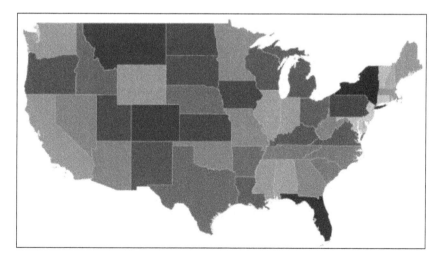

The shape is calculated by converting the `CENSUSAREA` field value to a hex number and then prefixing it to make it a fixed length.

Index

A

ActionSheet widget
  about 130
  used, for displaying list of actions 150-153
activate event 86
advance charting widgets
  used, for data visualization 193
aggregate functions
  avg function 183
  count function 183
  first function 183
  max function 183
  min function 183
  used, to display data on charts 181-184
Ajax
  used, for loading content of modal
      window 104
  used, for loading PanelBar content 83-86
Application object
  used, for navigating between multiple
      views 121-125
autoUpload property 95
avg function 183

B

barcode image
  generating, various encoding methods
      used 207, 208
built-in Validator
  used, for validating user input 19-22

C

cancel event handler 99
center method 108
charts
  binding, to DataSource object 173-175
  creating, kendoChart function used 168, 169
  creating to display data, aggregate functions
      used 181-184
  default theme, modifying 172, 173
  legend information position, modifying 171
  making interactive, event handlers
      used 185-188
  multiaxis chart, creating 177-181
  multiple categories, displaying 170
  multiple series, displaying 175
  title position, modifying 171
  values, displaying 176, 177
charts, options
  categoryAxis option 169
  series option 169
  title option 169
  valueAxis option 169
chart type
  changing, dynamically 188-192
checkbox
  used, for selecting nodes in TreeView 58-61
click event handler 107
client-side templates
  used, for generating HTML markup 8-11
close method 108
complete event handler 99
connect function 213

Content Delivery Network (CDN) 8
contentLoad event 86
content, PanelBar
  loading, Ajax used 83-86
contentUrls property 84
count function 183
custom aggregator function 183
customization, PanelBar 88, 89
customization, Window 105-108

D

data
  displaying, in Grid 28-32
  displaying in Grid, filters used 35-38
  sorting, in Grid 32-35
data-bind attribute 18, 189
data binding
  creating, MVVM used 12-16
  used, for generating HTML content 16-19
data-icon attribute 133
data-id attribute 113
data-layout attribute 114
data-role attribute 113, 131
DataSource component 28
DataSource object
  about 29, 52
  charts, binding to 173-175
  ListView widget, binding to 134-136
  PanelBar, binding to 86, 88
dataSource property 138
data-style attribute 132
dataTextField attribute 54
data-transition attribute
  about 125
  fade 126
  overlay 126
  slide 125
  zoom 125
DataViz (data visualization)
  about 167
  with advance charting widgets 193
delete command 39
display of list items
  customizing, template used 93, 94
Django 8
doubletap event 128

drag-and-drop
  used, for moving elements in TreeView 55-58
  used, for uploading files 97

E

edit command 39
editing
  in Grid 39
  inline 39
  popup 39
Editor
  about 65
  image browser tool used, for inserting
    images 70-76
Editor toolset
  tools, adding in 67-70
  tools, removing in 67-70
endless scrolling list
  building, ListView widget used 148-150
error event handler 86, 99
event handlers
  used, for making charts interactive 185-188
exec function 70
expand event 86

F

field property 29
files
  uploading asynchronously, file uploader
    used 94-96
  uploading, drag-and-drop used 97
  uploading synchronously, file uploader
    used 91-93
file uploader
  about 91
  file upload events, listening 98, 99
  localizing 97
  used, for uploading files
    asynchronously 94-96
  used, for uploading files synchronously 91-93
file upload events
  cancel event handler 99
  complete event handler 99
  error event handler 99
  listening 98, 99

progress event handler 99
remove event handler 99
select event handler 99
success event handler 99
upload event handler 99
filters
used, for displaying data in Grid 35-38
first function 183
fixed headers
creating, ListView widget used 137-139
fixedHeaders property 138
flow diagrams
creating, Kendo Diagram used 211-215

G

GeoJSON 225
getKendoDiagram function 211
Grid
about 23
creating, to display tabular data 23-27
customizing 46-48
data displaying, filters used 35-38
data, displaying in 28-32
data, sorting in 32-35
records, creating 39-43
records, deleting 39-43
records, updating 39-43
virtualization, using 43-45
group property 138

H

Handlebars 8
hash templates 8
hasModels property 144
hierarchical list
building, ListView widget used 143-147
hierarchical structural diagrams
creating, layout option used 215-220
hold event 128
href attribute 131
HTML content
generating, data binding used 16-19
HTML markup
generating, client-side templates used 8-11
http method 41

I

icons
using with nodes, in TreeView 62, 63
id property 144
image browser tool
used, for inserting images into Editor 70-76
images
inserting into Editor, image browser tool
used 70-76
initial layout
setting, during application
initialization 117-121
initial view
setting, during application
initialization 117-121
inline editing 39
inserthtml command 70
items array 69

J

Jade 8
Java Server Pages 8

K

kendoChart function
used, for creating charts 168, 169
Kendo Diagram
used, for creating flow diagrams 211-215
kendoDiagram function
connectionDefaults option 211
endCap option 211
startCap option 211
kendoEditor function
about 66
used, for creating WYSIWYG Editor 65, 66
kendoMap function 220
kendoMobileListView function 135
kendoRadialGauge function
endAngle option 200
pointer option 200
startAngle option 200
kendoStockChart function 195
Kendo UI
application framework 7
data visualization 167

Editor 65
file uploader 91
Grid 23
Mobile framework 111
Mobile widgets 129
PanelBar 77
TreeView 49
Window 101

Kendo UI application framework
client-side templates used, for generating
HTML markup 8-11
data binding, creating with MVVM 12-16
data binding used, for generating HTML
content 16-19
user input validating, built-in Validator
used 19-22

kendoValidator method 22

L

labels option 176
layout
creating, for mobile application 112-116
layout option, kendoDiagram function
left subtype 217
mindmapHorizontal subtype 217
mindmapVertical subtype 217
radial subtype 217
right subtype 217
tipOver subtype 217
up subtype 217
used, for creating hierarchical structural
diagrams 215-220
Linear Gauge widget
creating 205-207
list
creating, ListView widget used 130-134
list elements
filtering, ListView widget used 139-143
ListView widget
about 130-134
binding, to DataSource object 134-136
list elements, filtering 139-143
used, for building endless scrolling
list 148-150
used, for building hierarchical list 143-147

used, for creating fixed headers 137-139
used, for creating list 130-134

M

map
creating, OpenStreet map used 220-224
creating, that is bound to GeoJSON
data 225-227
maximize method 108
min function 183
minimize method 108
Mobile framework
about 111
initial layout, setting 117-121
initial view, setting 117-121
layout, creating for mobile
application 112-116
multiple views, navigating between 121-125
touch events, adding to mobile
application 126-128
views, adding to layout 112-116
Mobile library. *See* **Mobile widgets**
mobileListViewInit function 138
Mobile widgets
about 129
ActionSheet widget 129
ListView widget 129
Navbar widget 129
ScrollView widget 129
SplitView widget 130
TabStrip widget 129
modal window
configuring, to display pop up 102, 103
content loading, Ajax used 104
differentiating, with Window 102
displaying, on click of button 103, 104
Model View Controller. *See* **MVC**
Model View Presenter. *See* **MVP**
Model View ViewModel. *See* **MVVM**
multiaxis chart
creating 177-181
multiple file uploads
disabling 93
multiple views
navigating between, Application object
used 121-125

Mustache 8
MVC 12
MVP 12
MVVM
  about 12
  used, for creating data binding 12-16

N

name property 69
navigate method 123

O

onChangeHandler function 191
open method 104, 108
OpenStreet map
  used, for creating map 220-224
operators object 38

P

PanelBar
  about 77
  binding, to DataSource object 86, 88
  content loading, Ajax used 83-86
  creating 77-82
  customizing 88, 89
path parameter 73
pin method 108
popup editing 39
position attribute 105
progress event handler 99

Q

Quick Response code (QR code)
  about 209
  generating 209, 210

R

Radial Gauge widget
  creating 199, 200
  majorUnit value, specifying 200, 201
  minorUnit value, specifying 200, 201
  pointer value, updating with Slider
    widget 204, 205

radial color, specifying with ranges
    option 202, 203
refresh method 108
remove event handler 99
removeUrl property 95
restore method 108

S

saveUrl property 95
scale attribute
  ranges option 202
ScrollView widget
  about 130
  used, for navigating through collection of
    pictures 153-156
select event handler 86, 99
select tag 17, 18
setOptions function 191
setStatusClass function 56
Smarty 8
SplitView widget
  about 130
  creating, to build interaction between multiple
    panes 157-162
  creating, to display multiple panes 157-162
spriteCssClass property 62
statusClass property 56
Stock chart
  about 194
  creating, to show stock history 194-197
  date range, specifying 197, 198
  navigator pane, customizing 198, 199
styles directory 25
success event handler 99
swipe event 128

T

TabStrip widget
  used, for navigating between views 163-165
tap event 128
template
  used, for customizing display of list
    items 93, 94
template property 136, 138
text property 69

title property 29, 105
toggleMaximization method 108
tools
  adding, in Editor toolset 67-70
  removing, in Editor toolset 67-70
touch events
  adding to mobile application 126-128
touchstart event 128
TreeView
  about 49
  constructing, from remote DataSource
      object 52-54
  creating, to display directory structure 49-52
  elements moving, drag and drop used 55-58
  icons, using with nodes 62, 63
  nodes selecting, checkbox used 58-61
type attribute 71

U

underscore.js 8
unpin method 108
upload event handler 99
uploadUrl attribute 74
user input
  validating, built-in Validator used 19-22

V

value property 69
ViewModel object 13, 17
views
  adding, to layout 112-116
  navigating between, TabStrip widget
      used 163-165
  transition effect, specifying 125, 126
virtualization
  using, in Grid 43-45

W

What-You-See-Is-What-You-Get interface. *See*
      WYSIWYG interface
Window
  about 101
  customization 105-108
  differentiating, with modal window 102
  modal window configuring, to display pop
      up 102, 103
Window API
  using, to act on window object 108-110
WYSIWYG Editor
  creating, kendoEditor function used 65, 66
WYSIWYG interface 65

Thank you for buying
Kendo UI Cookbook

About Packt Publishing

Packt, pronounced 'packed', published its first book "*Mastering phpMyAdmin for Effective MySQL Management*" in April 2004 and subsequently continued to specialize in publishing highly focused books on specific technologies and solutions.

Our books and publications share the experiences of your fellow IT professionals in adapting and customizing today's systems, applications, and frameworks. Our solution based books give you the knowledge and power to customize the software and technologies you're using to get the job done. Packt books are more specific and less general than the IT books you have seen in the past. Our unique business model allows us to bring you more focused information, giving you more of what you need to know, and less of what you don't.

Packt is a modern, yet unique publishing company, which focuses on producing quality, cutting-edge books for communities of developers, administrators, and newbies alike. For more information, please visit our website: www.packtpub.com.

About Packt Open Source

In 2010, Packt launched two new brands, Packt Open Source and Packt Enterprise, in order to continue its focus on specialization. This book is part of the Packt Open Source brand, home to books published on software built around Open Source licenses, and offering information to anybody from advanced developers to budding web designers. The Open Source brand also runs Packt's Open Source Royalty Scheme, by which Packt gives a royalty to each Open Source project about whose software a book is sold.

Writing for Packt

We welcome all inquiries from people who are interested in authoring. Book proposals should be sent to author@packtpub.com. If your book idea is still at an early stage and you would like to discuss it first before writing a formal book proposal, contact us; one of our commissioning editors will get in touch with you.

We're not just looking for published authors; if you have strong technical skills but no writing experience, our experienced editors can help you develop a writing career, or simply get some additional reward for your expertise.

Learning Kendo UI
Web Development

ISBN: 978-1-84969-434-6   Paperback: 288 pages

An easy-to-follow practical tutorial to add exciting features to your web pages without being a JavaScript expert

1. Learn from clear and specific examples on how to utilize the full range of the Kendo UI tool set for the web.

2. Add powerful tools to your website supported by a familiar and trusted name in innovative technology.

3. Learn how to add amazing features with clear examples and make your website more interactive without being a JavaScript expert.

Instant Kendo UI Mobile

ISBN: 978-1-84969-911-2   Paperback: 60 pages

Practical recipes to learn the Kendo UI Mobile library and its various components for building mobile applications effectively

1. Learn something new in an Instant! A short, fast, focused guide delivering immediate results.

2. Understand the various components on the Kendo UI Mobile application framework.

3. Learn to use the various widgets in the Kendo UI Mobile library that will help you build a mobile application rapidly.

4. Build applications that provide native look and feel without having to maintain a separate code base.

Please check **www.PacktPub.com** for information on our titles

Building Mobile Applications Using Kendo UI Mobile and ASP.NET Web API

ISBN: 978-1-78216-092-2   Paperback: 256 pages

Get started with Kendo UI Mobile and learn how to integrate it with HTTP-based services built using ASP.NET Web API

1. Learn the basics of developing mobile applications using HTML5 and create an end-to-end mobile application from scratch.

2. Discover all about Kendo UI Mobile, ASP .NET Web API, and how to integrate them.

3. Understand how to organize your JavaScript code to achieve extensibility and maintainability.

Instant Kendo UI Grid

ISBN: 978-1-84969-913-6   Paperback: 56 pages

Learn an amazing JavaScript framework that will boost the look and function of your tabular data

1. Learn something new in an Instant! A short, fast, focused guide delivering immediate results.

2. Understand how to allow users to manipulate data.

3. Learn how to make large datasets easy to manage and filter.

4. Discover how to dress up tables to make them look more appealing.

Please check **www.PacktPub.com** for information on our titles

www.ingramcontent.com/pod-product-compliance
Lightning Source LLC
Chambersburg PA
CBHW060541060326
40690CB00017B/3567